SUSSEX AI IN THE SECOND WORLD WAR

Robin J. Brooks

COUNTRYSIDE BOOKS
NEWBURY, BERKSHIRE

First Published 1993
© Robin J. Brooks 1993
Reprinted 1996, 1998, 2000

COUNTRYSIDE BOOKS
3 Catherine Road
Newbury, Berkshire

To view our complete range of books,
please visit us at
www.countrysidebooks.co.uk

ISBN 1 85306 259 6

The cover painting is from an original watercolour
by Roland Davies and is reproduced by kind permission
of J. Salmon & Co. Ltd., fine art publishers of Sevenoaks.

Designed by Mon Mohan

Produced through MRM Associates Ltd., Reading
Typeset by Paragon Typesetters, Queensferry
Printed in England

CONTENTS

over

INTRODUCTION

Like its neighbouring county of Kent, Sussex suffered a lot from the effects of the Second World War. One of the principal towns, Eastbourne, was to gain the reputation of the most raided town in the South East though this is subject to scrutiny. It was, however, the first town in Sussex to witness at first hand the grim realities of war. The county hosted many airfields to combat the might of the German war machine, poised just across the Channel, ready to invade these islands. 'Operation Sealion', the name Hitler gave to the intended invasion, did not take place and the Battle of Britain was fought and won above the skies of this and several other counties.

The memories of the airfields are slowly dwindling as the men and women who served and flew from the Sussex sites become a dying breed. This and the fact that the majority of the airfields are now being used for other purposes mean that to a new generation they can only be read about in the few history books giving details of the airfields.

In this book I have tried to bring together the stories of all the Sussex airfields whether large or small. From the big operational stations such as Tangmere and Thorney to the small Advanced Landing Grounds that served only for several months, they are all part of the county's heritage. I have always felt a passion for the Sussex airfields and have studied all of them in some detail. They all have tales of courage and devotion attached to them. For the intrepid aviation historian, there are still signs to be found of action on all the sites, and the Robertsbridge Aviation Museum together with the Tangmere Military Aviation Museum are veritable treasure troves of information concerning the county's war. Civil Aviation is still pre-dominant at Shoreham Airport and long may this remain, for today it seems as though every airfield site is looked upon as a future industrial estate. Is it really too much to hope that future generations may be left a little of the past to ponder upon?

Robin J. Brooks

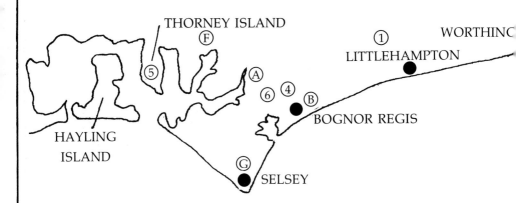

THORNEY ISLAND
(F)

WORTHING

(5)

(1)
LITTLEHAMPTON

(A)

(6) (4)

(B)

HAYLING
ISLAND

BOGNOR REGIS

(G)

SELSEY

(D)

KEY TO AIRFIELDS

1. FORD
2. FRISTON
3. SHOREHAM
4. TANGMERE
5. THORNEY ISLAND
6. WESTHAMPNETT

KEY TO ALGs & MLG

A. APULDRAM
B. BOGNOR
C. CHAILEY
D. COOLHAM
E. DEANLAND
F. FUNTINGTON
G. SELSEY
H. HAMMERWOOD (MINOR
   LANDING GROUND)

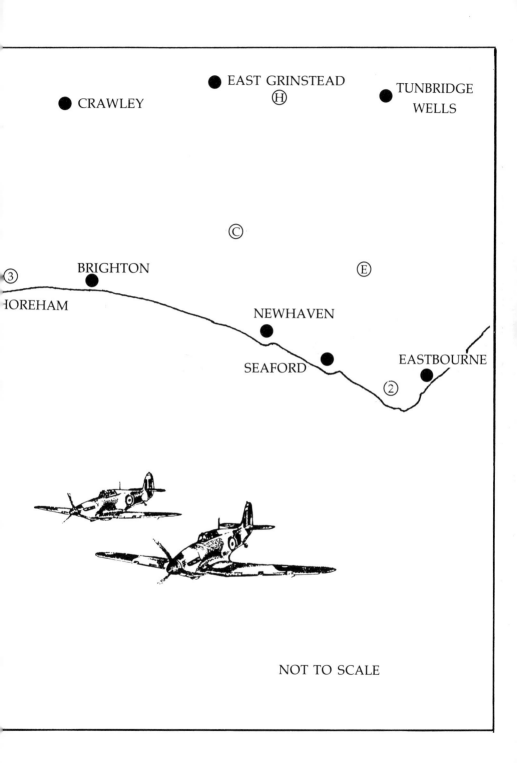

NOT TO SCALE

I

SETTING
THE SCENE

The Royal Naval Air Service and the Royal Flying Corps went into the First World War equipped with unarmed biplanes. They were used mainly for reconnaissance but as the war progressed they were in demand for other purposes. By 1916 the introduction of single seat fighters had turned the aircraft into a killing machine, but with the armistice in November 1918, the quick demobilising of men ensured a rapid reduction in fighting aircraft. No-one thought that war on such a scale would be repeated. Hitler's rise to power in Germany and the systematic demolition of the Versailles Treaty changed this pattern. The slide to another global war came even closer when Italy began hostilities against Abyssinia in 1935 even though their treachery was condemned by the League of Nations. Sanctions against Italy only brought a Rome-Berlin pact culminating in the Spanish Civil War where Italy and Germany supported General Franco and Russia supported the Spanish Government.

This war lasted for 2½ years and proved an excellent training ground for the air and land forces of both Italy and Germany. For Britain, hopelessly under-equipped and unfit for another major war, it was none too soon to begin to rebuild its forces. In the case of the RAF, it was fortunate that in 1932 the Air Ministry had been allowed to issue a specification for a high speed, multi-gun fighter to be used for air defence. This resulted in the production of the Hurricane and later the Spitfire. The ban on development of heavy bombers was also lifted three years later enabling a specification for a long range twin engined bomber to be issued, resulting in the Handley Page Hampden and the Vickers Wellington.

In 1935 Hitler had introduced conscription in Germany, and when one year later his troops marched into the Rhineland, a zone that had been demilitarised under the Versailles Treaty to provide France with a buffer against attack it became obvious that another war was looming. Though these moves were deplored in Britain little was done to prevent them and no real urgency was apparent in the build-up of the RAF, for these were still the halcyon days of flying. The growth of the German war machine was not fully appreciated until two ministers, Sir John Simon and Mr Anthony Eden, visited the country in 1935. Shocked at what they saw they realised that the fighting strength of Britain was indeed low and a big expansion of the armed forces began.

In 1936 the Home Defence force stood at 42 RAF squadrons with several more stationed abroad. Obviously these were quite inadequate for the conduct of a full-scale war and so 33 volunteer reserve centres were established together with Elementary Flying Training schools and later on the Civil Air Guard. The old ADGB (Air Defence of Great Britain) was disbanded and the system reorganised on four different Commands: Fighter, Bomber, Coastal, and Training. At the same time the RAF relinquished control of the Fleet Air Arm to the Navy and formed three new Commands: Maintenance, Balloon, and Reserve.

These moves were none too soon as the first crisis in the run-down to war began with the country being brought to the brink in September 1938, caused by the intention of Hitler to occupy the Sudetenland, officially belonging to Czechoslovakia. France and Britain threatened to go to war against Germany if he carried out this threat. We were however too hopelessly weak to attempt any sort of war and therefore accepted a compromise solution at the Munich meeting. Although Prime Minister Neville Chamberlain guaranteed us 'peace for our time', the country knew that it was to be a very uneasy peace.

It did not last long, and when war broke out on the 3rd September 1939 Britain was still not ready. The delay of eight months until Hitler invaded Western Europe did however enable the RAF to double its fighter strength. It also enabled the chain of radar stations to become fully operational, the Observer Corps to become fully trained and the

Rye early warning Radar Station, dismantled in 1958 (Kent Messenger).

anti-aircraft guns to be further deployed. Had we not had this period of inactivity known as the 'Phoney War', the outcome of the war may have been entirely different.

It was already realised that Sussex, like Kent, would bear the brunt of the initial German assault. Early warning radar stations had been built at Rye, Fairlight, Pevensey, Beachey Head, Truleigh and Poling. Tangmere had become a sector or controlling station within No. 11 Group, Fighter Command. Westhampnett became a satellite of Tangmere and a fighter airfield in its own right. Friston, high on the cliffs, was well placed as a forward satellite airfield and during the battle was to be used by many aircraft in distress, bombers as well as fighters. Shoreham, already a well known civil airport, was requisitioned by the Air Ministry at the height of the battle whilst Ford, a naval air station, was brought into the arena after a bad attack by the Luftwaffe on 18th August. Coastal Command was already established at Thorney Island when the onslaught began and due to faulty German intelligence, suffered badly at the hands of the enemy (see Chapter Four). There were other airfields in the county which were not primarily in use during the Battle of Britain but whose glory came later in the war and it is right that they too should be mentioned.

So the scene was set for the greatest aerial battle of all time. The Luftwaffe, proud of its achievements so far, was committed to destroying Fighter Command. To achieve this, Reichsmarschall

11

The plaque commemorating the birth of Thorney Island Airfield (Portsmouth Publishing and Printing).

Hermann Goering, Commander-in-Chief of the Luftwaffe, assembled three huge air fleets. Luftflotten 2 commanded by Feldmarschall Albert Kesselring in Holland, Luftflotten 3 commanded by Feldmarschall Hugo Sperle in Northern France and Luftflotten 5 under General Hans-Juergen Stumpff in Norway and Denmark. The combined strength of Luftflotten 2 and 3 amounted to some 900 Messerschmitt 109 and 110 fighters, 875 Heinkel HE 111, Junkers JU 88 and Dornier 17 bombers with 300 Junkers JU 87 'Stuka' dive-bombers. Not so powerful, though nonetheless potent, came Luftflotten 5 with 123 bombers and 34 ME 110 fighters. Against this formidable force the RAF was only able to muster 46 squadrons of Hurricanes and Spitfires and two squadrons of Boulton Paul Defiants, a total of somewhere between 600 and 700 single engined fighters. The odds were overwhelmingly uneven!

The Battle itself was divided into five particular phases. Initially Channel shipping and coastal ports were the targets. Then came the

Women played an essential role in World War Two. Here two WAAFs cheerfully plot the movements of aircraft (South Eastern Newspapers).

offensive against coastal airfields and radar stations followed by attacks on the inland airfields. The fourth phase saw London as the main target and fighter/bomber attacks on secondary targets were deemed the final phase. Historians now regard the Battle of Britain as beginning on Wednesday 10th July and finishing on 31st October 1940. It claimed a terrible loss of life, both British and German. In the case of the RAF, whilst the original estimate counted only fighter command pilots killed in the Battle, that number being 375, in March 1947 the estimate was enlarged to include pilots from every command including those of the Fleet Air Arm who lost their lives between the official days of the Battle of Britain, bringing the total to 1,503.

For Sussex as with the rest of the country, it was a traumatic time. With much of the opening phase taking place over the Channel around the Sussex coastline, it fell to the county to claim one of the first disasters of the war. It took place off Eastbourne on the 20th March 1940 when the SS *Barn Hill* was on route from Halifax to London. She was attacked by a lone raider shortly after 10.30 pm and hit by a string of bombs. One penetrated the deck and exploded in the hold killing four crew members. Several other boats in the vicinity came to her rescue including the Eastbourne lifeboat which managed to rescue the remainder of the crew. Shortly after this, the *Barn Hill* broke her back and was beached at Langney Point near Eastbourne where she became the subject of further attention from the Luftwaffe and much looting by the local people. The ship went into history books as the first to be lost in the Channel bombings. It also was the first incident of war for the county and indicated that the onslaught of the enemy would be directed over and around Sussex. The following chapters will go some way to retell those dramatic times.

Many of the Sussex airfields came into existence during the First World War. Some were operated by the RNAS and some by the RFC, with both of them flying flimsy canvas-covered machines in defence of the realm. Within the four years of the war, however, air power was well on the way to becoming the crucial factor in warfare. Prior to this the army had frowned upon the use of such machines condemning them purely to reconnaissance operations. The French General Foch had said 'Aviation is a good sport but for the army it is useless.' Time was to prove that this was not so.

The machines used by the British at the outbreak of the first conflict were varied and mainly from civilian manufacturers. Names like the

14

Maurice Farman Longhorn, Bristol Boxkite, Short S45 and Sopwith Tabloid became very familiar and whilst awe-inspiring in size, they did very little in the way of defence or attack. It was the airships that initially went to war in 1914, these being mainly operated by the RNAS. With experiments beginning in the early 1900s the outbreak of war saw very few ships actually in service. What few were available were used on coastal patrol duties. When the enemy submarines became a menace, the Admiralty quickly ordered the construction of non-rigid airships known as 'Blimps'. These were later assigned to convoy escort duties and played a crucial rôle in keeping our Channel sealanes open. The real fighters of the First World War did not really come along until 1917 and 1918. When they did they proved very capable of matching the German supremacy in fighter aircraft.

For Sussex, the year 1917 seems to have marked a significant period in the development of the airfields. As the upsurge in enemy U-boat activity in the Channel came about following the German declaration of unrestricted submarine warfare, so more bases close to the Channel were needed. One of the earliest airfields to open and one that was not operated by the RNAS during the war but by the RFC, was Shoreham.

First established in 1911 as a civilian airfield, it was the Brooklands to Brighton Air Race in May of that year that placed Shoreham on the aviation map. Running alongside a railway embankment, it had a good size landing run and was officially opened shortly after by the Mayors of Brighton, Hove and Worthing as a municipal airport. It participated in the Circuit of Europe Air Race and recorded the first cargo flight in the world when a consignment of Osram lamps was flown in.

During 1913/14, the Sussex County Aero Club was established at the airfield but enthusiasm was very limited. The site was acquired by the War Office in August 1914 and taken over by the RFC a short time later. Though designated a training field it was not until early 1915 that No. 3 Reserve Aeroplane Squadron arrived equipped with several Longhorns. Great was the thrill one day when a brand new BE 2C landed at Shoreham. The pilots and ground-crews of the resident squadron gathered around in awe of this beautiful aircraft and its test pilot who, during lunch in the mess, discussed its flying capabilities and technical merits with all and promised a flying

Airships were increasingly used by the Admiralty in World War One. Here a Polegate based Scout Zero 30 is on submarine spotting duty over the Channel (A. Saunders Collection).

demonstration for the afternoon. Donning a lot of leather clothing, the pilot and his passenger, a technical scientist, strapped themselves in. Taking off steeply, the aircraft flew along the line of the railway line until the spectators on the ground heard the cough of a starved engine. Staring intently they saw the nose of the aircraft drop as the pilot, realising he had lost power, turned back for the airfield. Trying to maintain height, he stalled over the newly built aircraft sheds and dived into the ground. Sadly both pilot and passenger died in the flames and the entire tragedy brought home the fact that flying in those days was a very risky business.

No. 1 Wing of the CAF arrived after the armistice and stayed until 1921 when the airfield was returned to civilian use. It was again used by the military in the prewar expansion period of the RAF by No. 16 E & RFTS flying Tiger Moths. With war imminent they left on the 1st September 1939 whereupon Shoreham continued in civil use until June 1940 when it was totally requisitioned by the Air Ministry.

The year 1917 also saw Tangmere established as an airfield although it came to the attention of the military by way of a journalist, Geoffrey Dorman, making an emergency landing whilst en route to Gosport. Two hundred acres were finally requisitioned in September 1917 when a party of German POWs were drafted in to begin ground work. Whilst building was going on, No. 92 Squadron flew their SE 5As in for training purposes in March 1918 followed later by No. 61 with Avro 504s and Bristol F2 Bs. The field was allocated to the Americans in September 1918, by which time the RAF had been formed from the RNAS and the RFC with Sussex being included in the No. 1 area together with Kent and Berkshire. The armistice prevented any real American operation from Tangmere and it reverted to a holding station for squadrons returning from the continent.

Closed in 1920, the site was retained by the Air Ministry and with an SHQ being activated on 23rd November 1926, No. 43 Squadron with Gloster Gamecocks arrived followed by No. 1 equipped with

Fragile looking De Havilland 60G Moths at Ford Airfield c. 1932 (Southdowns Aero Club).

Siskin IIIAs. Around this period Tangmere became known as the best fighter station in the country. Situated as it was close to the south coast and Brighton with its obvious attractions, every squadron in the RAF wanted a posting there! The next ten years were very tranquil, but with the expansion period in 1937 many squadrons came and went. With the Munich crisis in 1938, the airfield prepared for yet another war and although not known at the time, the name of Tangmere was to become as well known as Biggin Hill.

In very close proximity to Tangmere was Ford. Like the former, the site was authorised as a training station in 1917 and German POWs started work early in 1918. Again like Tangmere, it was earmarked for use by the United States Air Service who intended to fly the Handley Page 0/400 bomber during 1918. This did not materialise and the first squadron to arrive at Ford was No. 148 of the RFC who flew FE 2B bombers. The Americans did arrive later but the field reverted to the RAF early in 1918 then closed in January 1920. It was ten years before flying returned and then mainly in the civil rôle. Sir Alan Cobham used Ford extensively during his National Aviation Day campaign until it was requisitioned by the Admiralty and commissioned as HMS Peregrine. In use by the Navy during the opening phases of the war as a training airfield, Ford did not go unnoticed by the Luftwaffe who delivered a devastating attack on it during the Battle of Britain. It reverted to RAF control in September 1940 and found a new rôle as an experimental airfield for the Fighter Interception Unit. In addition to this, many squadrons used Ford whilst carrying the war back to Germany and it reverted back to the Navy in September 1945. It became famous once again for its peacetime naval open days until final closure in 1958.

Another airfield with naval connections was Thorney Island, although this came under the control of Coastal Command. Building did not begin until 1935 and was intended to be finished by 1937. However, with several delays and lack of civilian co-operation, it was not completed until 1938. The outbreak of war saw Blenheims operating from Thorney on reconnaissance and fighter duties, and like Ford the airfield suffered badly from attacks during 1940. One of the most famous operations of the war code-named 'Operation Fuller' was to include Beauforts from Thorney Island. The eventual almost safe passage of the German battle fleet through the Dover Straits had its repercussions long after the event (see Chapter Four).

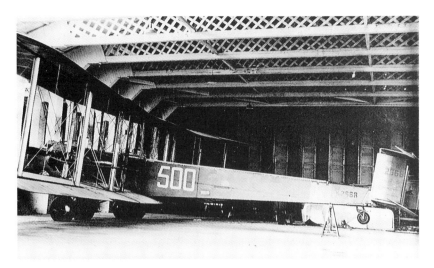

A Vickers Aircraft undergoing repairs at Ford in 1934 (Richard Riding).

A period in Fighter Command and then as a transport base allowed Thorney Island to continue flying until 1976 when it was axed in a defence review.

Although designated a satellite airfield to Tangmere, Westhampnett was to prove one of the busiest bases in the county during the Battle. Approved by the Air Ministry as an ELG (Emergency Landing Ground) for Tangmere in 1938, it was ready for action when the Battle of Britain commenced. Built on part of the Goodwood estate, during the 1950s it became rather well known for its car racing circuit. Turning full circle it has reverted to flying and is now a popular venue for light aircraft.

Of the remaining airfields in Sussex, only Friston saw action during the Battle. Originally a private landing ground known as either East Dean or Gayles, it was in use in 1936 as a landing ground for several Army Co-operation units based in Sussex and the neighbouring counties. Sitting high on the Seven Sisters cliffs near Eastbourne, it was very often the first airfield seen by aircraft returning from dogfights over the Channel and was therefore very much in use as an ELG. Later in the war, stricken bombers returning would use the field and it became quite common to see B.17s, Lancasters and others sitting around its perimeter in various stages of distress. No resident

19

squadrons were based at Friston until well after the Battle of Britain but it is worthy of mention in this book.

For the rest of the Sussex airfields, their claim to fame came in the years following the Battle of Britain. Merston near Chichester was intended to be ready for July 1940 and was designated another satellite to Tangmere. Although surveyed in early 1939, it was not open until March 1941 and thus missed the crucial period but it was in use constantly from then on until the end of the war. The county saw the build-up of ALGs (Advanced Landing Grounds) during 1943 and by the time D Day had arrived, seven were operational. Most of them were planned for completion by spring 1943 but problems with permission from landowners, bad weather, clearance of sites and bad drainage all led to delays. Built by Army and RAF construction gangs, they served their purpose admirably as forward bases prior to the invasion. After D Day they were strangely quiet as the units moved over the Channel to France. They were subsequently derequisitioned and returned to their respective landowners but several in Sussex were intent on continuing flying.

Most notable in this category are Deanland and Bognor. The former was occupied by Polish squadrons in the run-up to D Day whilst Bognor became a Norwegian ALG. Today Deanland, also known as Ripe, is privately owned but is available for landings to light aircraft with prior permission. Bognor is also in constant use and is operated and maintained by LEC Refrigeration. The rest of the ALGs have returned to agriculture although signs of them are still visible.

Some of the Sussex airfields not relevant to this book are now long gone but had their origins in the First World War. Goring-by-Sea was built in 1918 for the Americans but was never used, whilst Newhaven, a coastal port, saw considerable use by the RNAS. Rustington like Goring was built to house an American training squadron but the armistice stopped its use and not one aeroplane ever landed there. The same can be said for Southbourne whereas Telscombe Cliffs saw some action in the early conflict but is now totally developed as the town of Peacehaven. Eastbourne can claim to be the only town in the county ever to have manufactured aircraft but this lasted for a brief period only and very few signs remain today of this achievement. The only large airship base in Sussex existed at Polegate and this was the site of a tragic accident putting an end to its activities shortly after.

For a county rich in aviation sites, it is sad to think that only one airfield of considerable size continues to exist. Hopefully the future of Shoreham is assured. Of the rest, the history books are all that we have to remind us of the Battle of Britain period and what followed.

Airfield Buildings

By the end of the First World War there were supposedly 301 landing grounds in Britain. They were not of the size or type that were in use during the Battle of Britain but more like large fields in which had been erected canvas hangars, wooden huts and of course, tents. Most of them quickly returned to agriculture after 1918, so much so that by 1924 there were only 27 service and 17 civil airfields in the country. By 1935, with the 'new peace' becoming a little shaky, the Air Ministry Works Directorate was formed with the object of organising and planning the building of new airfields, with a budget of just under £5 million. From 1939 to 1941 the building continued with expenditure reaching its peak in 1942 at £145 million, an enormous amount of money for those days.

Work on the first of the new era of RAF stations began in 1935 with 11 sites being given priority. In Sussex, plans were drawn up to build a new airfield on Thorney Island with a large modernisation programme to be carried out at Tangmere. Most of the sites followed a circular layout with hangars, generally two or three, around the perimeter fairly close together. The accommodation and workshops together with technical buildings were usually within the same area to allow aircraft an unobstructed path when taking off and landing. Some preparation had taken place earlier with turf being laid and great consideration given to drainage which was essential on all grass airfields. As hard runways did not really materialise at many airfields until later in the war, some Battle of Britain airfields with bad drainage were forced to use metal planking on the grass. The tented living quarters had now given way to brick built units although these reverted to the former in 1944 when the ALGs were in operation. Tangmere became one of the first airfields to receive a hard runway after a decision taken by the Air Ministry in April 1939 that several fighter airfields were to be given priority. This was necessary to ensure all-weather usage at some of the front line airfields.

These early hard runways were of tarmac construction, not concrete, and as such were only strong enough for fighters to use. It was not considered safe to use them as dispersal areas overnight, or when flying was cancelled because of bad weather, in case the wheels sank into the tarmac. Dispersal was therefore only available around the perimeter of the airfields or in fields bordering the site. Later the dispersal areas became hard standing, but in 1940 neither the concrete nor the labour needed to build them were available. Speed was also important to get an airfield up and running whatever the lack of good facilities during this early period.

On the subject of dispersal areas, it was found necessary to provide some protection to the poor ground crews who had to service aircraft out in the open in all weathers. The answer came from a company called C Miskin and Sons who produced a prototype of the popular

Concrete replaced grass at many major airfields during 1942/3. The photograph shows a typical cross runway pattern (Imperial War Museum).

22

Blister hangar in early 1939. It was erected for trials at Biggin Hill in January 1940 and immediately proved a success with the long suffering ground crews. The original had canvas curtains at each end but as often as not these were left out or one end of the hangar was bricked up. Eventually over 3,000 Blisters were supplied to the RAF but most of these were removed from fighter airfields in 1942 and transferred to training airfields. By this time larger and better constructions known as Bellman hangars were used, and by late 1942 even these were being superseded by transportable sheds or T type hangars.

The question of fuel storage became an important issue in the planning of the airfields. It had long been decided that storage must be in some remote corner of the airfield and that each station should carry enough fuel for at least six weeks of intensive operations. In 1936 the average capacity at each airfield was around 48,000 gallons, usually contained in four 12,000 gallon tanks. It was then common practice for aircraft to taxi up to the compound and refuel. All of this changed when mobile fuel bowsers were introduced and fuel was taken to the aircraft, a practice that gave quicker refuelling in 1940.

The Blister hangar, barely adequate protection for working ground crews, first appeared in January 1940. A concrete Maycrete accommodation hut can be seen in the background (R.J. Brooks).

23

The basic layout for fuel dumps was usually three different locations in case of enemy attack, and the usual method of delivery to the airfield was by train and then lorry to the fuel dumps. The tanks were either sunk into the ground or built on the surface; in this case they would be protected by a brick surround. This method served the airfields well until 1941 when the Ministry of Fuel and Power built a series of pipelines to carry fuel to the larger airfields. This was the forerunner of the system known as PLUTO, Pipeline Under The Ocean, which in 1944 eventually piped fuel under the Channel direct to the advancing Allies.

It was also the domestic buildings that gave an airfield its character. With the big expansion of 1938/39, the Directorate of Public Works visited every single flying club at every single airfield within the British Isles. Some were chosen for upgrading to RAF stations and many of the buildings used by the flying clubs were ideal for domestic accommodation. Club houses were turned into billets overnight without of course the removal of the bar! With the need for further

Bleakly unwelcoming, Nissen huts such as this provided the comforts of home for many service personnel (R.J. Brooks)

buildings came the 'B' type wooden hut, but there was a shortage of wood around this period so various other types of huts were erected including the faithful Nissen hut, the Laing hut made of light timber, plasterboard and felt, and the concrete Maycrete hut. Several other designs were used later in the war but it is a measure of their general quality that many types are still standing and in use today for a variety of purposes.

Despite all of the forementioned building, it must be the tower that evokes more nostalgic feelings than any other associated with the 1940 period. The control tower is an American term that slowly replaced the general British one of watch tower. The control of RAF aircraft was non-existent until 1939 although many of the flying clubs used radio assistance. Watch towers became widely used during the Battle and were usually brick built adjacent to the hangar area. Some were even attached to the hangars themselves. As aircraft became

A forlorn reminder of Tangmere – the Control Tower as it is today (Portsmouth Publishing and Printing Ltd).

more sophisticated and airfields grew in size, so did the watch tower, and by 1941, the term control tower had taken over and the building had become a two or three storey brick built item with a panoramic view all over the airfield. The one classic example of a 1940 watch tower remains today at Westhampnett and later type control towers are still evident at Thorney Island and to a lesser degree, due to its deteriorating condition, at Tangmere. The rest have all disappeared together with many of the other buildings that made up the airfields of the Battle of Britain period.

The Defences

With the rapid advance of the German war machine throughout Europe, it was felt by the majority of the military that an invasion of Britain must be on Hitler's mind, but it was the total fall of France that altered entirely the strategic position with regard to the air defence of Britain. It is true that by 1939 certain defences had been put into place but it was thought that with the likelihood of an aerial invasion as well as seaborne one, the airfields of Sussex, without adequate protection, would be very vulnerable to a landing by paratroops. It was also imperative that they were adequately protected against attack and so with the Battle of Britain increasingly likely, early 1940 saw a rapid build-up of airfield defences. Pillboxes of various shapes and designs began to spring up around the airfield perimeters as well as in the surrounding countryside. Once again preparations were nearly too late.

It was not until February 1938 that the Government finally implemented a programme to bring the defences up to an acceptable level. This approved the provision of 1,264 heavy anti-aircraft (AA) guns and 4,728 searchlight units but it was to take until the beginning of the war to be fully realised. This was fine for the defence of major military installations and large cities but when it came to the defence of the airfields, facilities were sadly lacking.

On 11th July 1940, the 5th AA division which covered the south coast from Hastings to as far as Milford Haven had just four Bofors deployed at a Sussex airfield, that one being Tangmere. No other

Women equably faced the dangers of anti-aircraft defence. Here they manipulate height and range-finding equipment (Sussex Courier).

airfield in the county had at this period any major AA forms of defence. It was left to the individual stations to muster any guns they could and improvisation was the name of the game. The guns in the main were found to be either Lewis or Hispano machine guns and were sited in dugouts and strapped to various means of transport

27

either on the roof or on the side. These could obviously only deal with low flying raiders or a paratroop invasion; they were totally useless against high flying aircraft. The gun emplacements were originally dugouts in the ground but gradually purpose-built pillboxes became the norm with various designs known as Type 22 or 24 springing up on every airfield.

Many of the surface pillboxes at the Sussex airfields are around today, some still have the metal spigot in the middle upon which the gun was sited but all of them remain visible reminders of the Battle.

In the haste to defend the airfields after the outbreak of war the Air Ministry looked at any reasonable suggestion. One of the more curious ideas came from an inventor from Kent named Francis Norman Pickett. Though primarily an engineer and financier, he also dabbled in inventions, one of which placed him in the history books of the Second World War. Known as the 'Pickett-Hamilton Fort', it was a retractable or 'pop-up' pillbox that was sunk into the grass

The Pickett-Hamilton Fort was one of the more unusual inventions of World War Two. The photograph shows the pump mechanism by which pressure was created to raise the concrete circle containing the gunners (R.J. Brooks).

beside the main runway areas. The pillbox was circular, made of concrete and measuring some 6 ft in diameter. Inside this circular concrete was placed another smaller one thereby allowing it to move within the outer ring. A pumping device was inserted in the centre of the inner ring and this moved the pillbox up and down. Though very cramped inside, the fort was designed to be manned by two or three men equipped with either rifles or bren guns. Entering was via a metal hatch on top and the men, once inside, would fire their weapons through slits cut out of the inner section. Immediately after the action they would lower the fort to ground level thus denying the enemy the opportunity of firing back. Although seemingly a very far-fetched idea, it attracted the attention of Winston Churchill, who in the second volume of his war history records that he wrote to General Ismay on 12th July 1940 stating: 'I saw these pillboxes for the first time when I visited Langley Aerodrome last week. This [design] appears to afford an admirable means of anti-parachute defence and

Here, the hatch allows entry to a Pickett 'pop-up' turret; shown in its lowered position (R.J. Brooks).

it should surely be widely adopted. Let me have a plan.'

Work was started immediately and many of the airfields had received at least two by late August 1940. In Sussex, Tangmere was the only airfield to receive them and although quite a novel idea, they were never really used in anger. In fact there is no record of them being used at all except for the occasional false alarm. One of the main problems proved to be the constant flooding and the fact that men could not survive above 60 minutes in such enclosed and cramped conditions. The earliest version of the retractable fort was raised and lowered by a counter-balance but later types used either a compressed air cylinder or hand pump to raise and lower the active section. The raising mechanism was manufactured by various companies throughout the country, but the one thing they had in common was that they were all companies associated with agricultural engineering. British patent No. 491130 relates to the number stamped on the raising mechanism in the Tangmere fort and a copy of that number reveals that it is the complete specification to improvements relating to the raising and lowering of agricultural implements. This suggests that the whole affair of the forts was cloaked in secrecy and that rather than let the public, or indeed the enemy, know the true facts they were encompassed within a civilian specification. Donald Campbell of *Bluebird* fame allowed his own workshops to be used for the prototype build and he himself became very active during the development stage. Sadly the forts at Tangmere were removed when the MOD sold the land but one still remains today in the care of the Tangmere Military Aviation Museum, a vivid reminder of a very curious invention.

The same lack of success was achieved with the PAC rocket invention used for airfield defence. Installed at various airfields including Tangmere and it is thought Westhampnett, the Parachute and Cable device was intended to bring down enemy aircraft. Fired from a tube, the rockets would reach about 2,000 ft when two parachutes would be deployed automatically. The larger one would carry away the rocket case whilst the smaller parachute had a 1,000 ft length of cable attached to it with a small mine on the end. It was hoped that the cable would catch the wing of a bomber and drag the mine up to the aircraft with the obvious result. There is no record of it ever doing so, but again, it was an invention hastily brought into use for a country badly prepared for war.

The defence of the airfields was usually co-ordinated by a battle headquarters comprising both RAF and army personnel. Until the arrival of the RAF Regiment in 1943, the defence guns on airfields were manned by the army and one can imagine the rivalry that sprang up between the 'brylcreem boys' and the 'pongos'!! In June 1940 Churchill said: 'Every man in RAF uniform ought to be armed with something, a rifle, a tommy gun, a pistol, a pike or mace and everyone without exception should do at least one hour's drill and practice every day.' Whilst the last part of the statement did not go down too well, the battle itself saw a most unusual and extraordinary selection of weapons for airfield defence.

As the threat of invasion increased, almost all airfield personnel, male and female, were instructed in what to do if paratroops landed. Many were issued with or had access to side arms but with the knowledge that the enemy would be far better equipped and armed, this false sense of security was not very reassuring.

We cannot leave the question of defence without mentioning the searchlight units. It is little known that by 1936, 108 searchlight

To combat the threat of invasion various methods of hindering the enemy's advance were used. Here a barrier of oil drums effectively blocks the road to heavy transport (South Eastern Newspapers).

31

Frames of various shapes to deter aerial invasion were a common sight in Sussex fields (South Eastern Newspapers).

companies were in existence, mainly surrounding the cities of the UK. This was not considered enough by the Committee of Imperial Defence and it was suggested that the scale of defence should be increased. With Air Chief Marshal Sir Hugh Dowding taking the chair of the committee, the units had expanded to 456 by the time of the Munich crisis. Many by this time had sound locators enabling them to become more accurate when exposing the light, but still the committee insisted this was not enough and stated that London alone needed 1,056 searchlights for its defence. The winter of 1939/40 saw a rapid build-up of units and the formation of a new command called AA Command to combine the operations of the AA guns and the searchlights. By the time the Battle broke, 8,500 searchlights were operational, though not for the job of airfield defence. They did however assist aircraft in distress by pointing two or more beams towards the nearest airfield. Even better was the method known as the 'Sandra' lights which consisted of three searchlights placed on an airfield and when requested to do so, directing their beams upward to form a cone and thus help aircraft. Once the Battle was over, rapid

The royal family frequently visited the country's danger areas. In 1940 King George VI toured a defence position 'somewhere on the south coast' (South Eastern Newspapers).

advances were made in searchlight development, but during 1940 it was a very basic affair. Sussex became one of the more congested when it came to sites and women as well as men shared the duties on the searchlight units.

With the searchlight of course came the balloon. From 1940 they became a familiar sight over the wartime landscape and were used to prevent enemy aircraft from flying low and delivering their bombs with accuracy. They became known as 'gas bags' to the men and women who manned the sites which in Sussex during the Battle were very sparse. The only real effective balloon barrage was sited near Thorney Island and was intended for the defence of Portsmouth and Southampton.

Balloon Command was formed in 1938 by the newly integrated Air Council and it had been estimated then that 400 balloons would be needed for the London barrage with an indeterminate number elsewhere. Obviously defence of the Capital was of paramount

Barrage balloons, a common sight over the vulnerable areas of Britain, occasionally came to grief themselves. Unfortunately, as well as downing enemy aircraft and rocket missiles, in bad weather balloons also claimed British aircraft (South Eastern Newspapers).

importance but it was also felt that balloons stationed near the south east coast would at least stand a chance of bringing down an enemy aircraft before it travelled inland. The sites of aircraft production over here were also singled out for balloon protection but it is fair to say that during the Battle very few balloons were sited along the coast.

One of the first enemy aircraft to fall foul of a balloon was an HE 111 of KG 27 which struck a cable over Newport whilst returning from a raid over Merseyside on the 13th September 1940. Though this was towards the latter end of the Battle, it proved the system did work although the final number of aircraft that were brought down by this method was the subject of controversy after the war.

By far the greater use of the balloon barrage came during the V1 attacks which took place from June to September 1944. Although outside the scope of this book, many Sussex villages were damaged from crashing rockets and even the balloon sites themselves suffered impact damage. In 1945 a question was asked in Parliament as to whether the number of balloons used in the war was really effective or just a waste of manpower and resources. Whatever the real answer, they were certainly a memorable aspect of defence in the UK.

2
TANGMERE

Tangmere originated as an airfield during the First World War after a journalist, Geoffrey Dorman, force-landed there in 1916 and realised its potential as an airfield (see Chapter One). In the Second World War Tangmere was the sector or controlling station in sector 'A' of No. 11 Group, Fighter Command, covering an area stretching from west of Brighton to Portsmouth, Southampton and Bournemouth. During and after the Battle of Britain it became as well known as Biggin Hill and Kenley and was a fighter airfield up to the 1970s.

The tranquil years of 1926-1936 (see Chapter One) finished for Tangmere when the country became aware of the danger it faced from the build up of German military power and the airfield saw its first reformation of squadrons in 1937.

In 1938 another expansion programme of airfield buildings began as the war loomed ever closer. Barrack blocks, fuel dumps and living quarters sprang up overnight on most of the large airfields and Tangmere was no exception. The Munich crisis in 1938 brought about a dramatic change in attitude towards the potential enemy. At the airfield, air raid shelters were hastily dug, hangars were camouflaged and the Furies of both Squadrons 1 and 43 lost their shiny silver appearance as they were painted dark green and brown. It was all very ominous! At the same time a single Hawker Hurricane flew into Tangmere making the biplanes look suddenly obsolete. It stayed for only an hour, enough time for all the station personnel to see the future shape of the aeroplane. In the meantime, the training with the Furies was stepped up, reaching a peak before Neville Chamberlain returned from Germany in September. Although the crisis was over,

A 1937 mishap at Tangmere, when Flying Officer Anderson of 500 Squadron forgot to check his ballast (J. Wilson).

no-one really believed that the threat of war had been totally averted, but at least it was a much needed breathing space. It enabled the Fighter Control system to become even more efficient, the early warning Radar stations to be fully operational and most of all, time for the new aircraft to reach more squadrons.

Then came the bombshell that made war inevitable. On 23rd August 1939, the Germans and the Russians signed a treaty of non-aggression. Hitler and Stalin joined forces and Germany began its final preparations for the invasion of Poland. The British forces were once again put on full stand-by. Reservists in all three services were called up and general mobilisation was announced.

At Tangmere, No. 1 Squadron had received their new Hurricanes in October 1938, followed by 43 Squadron in November. Both squadrons worked up to full operational standard and with the station being designated a sector station within No. 11 Group of Fighter Command, the Ansons of 217 Squadron left for Warmwell. The 27th August saw Nos. 1 and 43 joined by an auxiliary unit, No. 605 (County of Warwick). Previously a bomber unit, it was

Hawker Furies over Tangmere. No. 43 Squadron practise formation flying during the Munich Crisis of 1938. The planes are camouflaged and their white and yellow roundels have no inner circles (Real Photos).

37

redesignated a fighter squadron and flew into Tangmere with a mixture of Gladiators and Hurricanes. The former were phased out by October and replaced by further Hurricanes. It was none too soon as in the early hours of 1st September 1939 Hitler's forces crossed the border into Poland. World War Two had begun.

Hurriedly No. 1 Squadron left for France on the 9th as part of the Advanced Striking Force and were replaced at Tangmere by a reformed 92 (East India) Squadron equipped with the first twin engined fighter to be seen at the airfield, the Bristol Blenheim. The airfield took on a distinctly warlike appearance as neatly painted white kerbstones were daubed in dark green paint and a high security fence was placed around the entire perimeter. Early in 1939 an asphalt perimeter track was laid in preparation for the new aircraft and at the same time, two grass runways running N/S and NE/SW were laid. Everyone waited for the onslaught.

It never happened, for this was to be the period known as the 'Phoney War'. In November, 43 took their Hurricanes to Acklington bidding a fond farewell to the airfield that had been home to them for eight years by beating up the airfield! ('Beating up the airfield' involved a very fast, very low fly-past of aircraft over the airfield that they were either leaving or arriving at: an act of bravado.) One week later they were replaced by 501 (County of Gloucester) Squadron of the Royal Auxiliary Air Force who flew their Hurricanes in from Filton. 501 had originally been named 'City of Bristol' but when it became embodied into the auxiliary air force from the Special Reserve in 1936, it changed its name to cover a larger area of potential recruitment.

Not a lot happened in the early part of 1940. It was a hard winter and much of the time was spent clearing snow. 92 had taken their Blenheims to Croydon just after Christmas Day but due to the bad weather the replacement Squadron, No. 601 (County of London) were grounded at Biggin Hill. The Squadron had acquired the name of 'Weekend Playboys' indicating that being auxiliaries, prior to mobilisation they had only flown at weekends. That however was all in the past and the Squadron, encouraged by their Commanding Officer Squadron Leader Brian Thynne, had put in many hours of training on the Blenheims to enable them to become as efficient as the Hurricane Squadrons. Although now commanded by Squadron Leader Noel Guiness, the same efficiency was brought to Tangmere

38

when the Squadron managed to leave Biggin Hill.

The New Year brought very little action and the fighting in France had little effect on the mundane routine of the airfield. It was known that this phoney period could not last for long and the Christmas and New Year celebrations were enjoyed by everyone to the full, for it was felt that it could be some time before a Christmas would be enjoyed again.

The 11th February 1940 saw 605 leave for Leuchars in Scotland as news of the fighting in France filtered through to Tangmere. The British Expeditionary Force and the Advanced Air Striking Force were suffering badly and many valuable Hurricanes had already been lost. France pleaded for more aircraft but by 19th May, Winston Churchill had decided against sending any more across the Channel. It further became abundantly clear that the RAF could not continue to operate from French airfields as the enemy pushed further towards the Channel ports. The remainder of the striking force flew back to Britain as the situation on the ground took its final turn. With the surrender of the Belgian army to the enemy, the BEF and the French 1st Army were pushed towards the Channel port of Dunkirk. This retreat culminated in 'Operation Dynamo', the Dunkirk evacuation. The date was 26th May 1940.

Just prior to 'Dynamo', 501 Squadron had been sent to Bethienville and a detachment of 601 to Merville in the fast fading hope of strengthening the BEF. They were replaced by No. 145 with Hurricanes who from 10th May were daily in action over the Dunkirk beaches. At the end of the month, 43 returned to Tangmere, glad to be back, and joined 145 in patrolling the beaches and coming into contact more and more with the enemy. As the pilots flew over the beachheads, they looked down upon what appeared to be a 'black swarm of ants', in reality an army in tatters. They saw the enemy aircraft, Junkers 87s, Messerschmitt 109s and 110s attacking the men on the sand, and tried valiantly to stop the slaughter. Sometimes the RAF fought out of sight of the army awaiting rescue and immediately the cry was 'Where the hell is the RAF?' Unfortunately the whole weight of air defence at Dunkirk fell on Fighter Command, and with the aircraft fighting out of range of any radar advance warning of enemy aircraft and at a considerable distance from their bases, it was inevitable that at times there were no aircraft in the sky. To indicate the number of operations, 28th May saw Fighter Command carry out

321 sorties against large German formations as the Royal Navy and the little ships struggled to bring the BEF back to England.

By 30th May bad weather had set in, bringing a badly needed break in enemy attacks, and 68,014 troops were rescued in one day. 'Operation Dynamo' was completed by 4th June but at a cost to Fighter Command of 320 pilots killed or missing and some 944 aircraft lost, both Hurricanes and Spitfires. The last squadron to leave France landed at Tangmere on the 13th June. No. 73 flew into the airfield before going on to Church Fenton. With France now occupied by the Germans, Britain stood alone to face a formidable enemy. The 'Phoney War' was over.

The Fighter Command Order of Battle for 7th July 1940 recorded that Tangmere had three Hurricane Squadrons in residence, Nos. 43, 145 and 601 together with the Fighter Interception Unit with Blenheims. It was the Germans' intention to establish air superiority over the Channel and close it to British shipping. Consequently the attacks from early July to early August, known as Phase One of the

Pilots of No. 43 Squadron stationed at Tangmere. During a sortie in July 1940 Sergeant Buck (left) drowned after his Hurricane was shot down in the Channel (Imperial War Museum).

Battle, were concentrated on convoys in the Channel Straits. It was considered by Goering to be a simple task, and accordingly, he only committed two Fliegerkorps to accomplish his objective. Based on the Pas-de-Calais was General Lorzer's II Fliegerkorps whilst at Le Havre was General Richthofen's VIII Fliegerkorps. Given the impression by his leader that clearing the English Channel was to be an easy task, Lorzer committed a small battle group under the command of Johannes Fink, Kommodore of the DO 17 Kampfgeschwader 2 based at Arras. Additional aircraft included two JU 87 'Stuka' gruppens and two ME 109 Jagdgeschwader also based along the Pas-de-Calais. Two of the fighter units were already notorious, for both were led by pilots of distinction – JG 26 by Major Adolf Galland and JG 23 by Major Werner Molders. Both were destined to become legends in the Luftwaffe.

The sector operations room at Tangmere had been fully operational since the beginning of the year and a satellite airfield had been built at nearby Westhampnett. It was as ready for the onslaught as it ever could be, and with historians now claiming that the Battle of Britain began on Wednesday 10th July 1940, the airfield began the most harrowing period of its history.

Thursday 11th July dawned a little overcast with cloud base at 5,000 ft. For many weeks prior to this the enemy units of Generals Lorzer and Richthofen had been attacking the coastal convoys with limited success but on this particular day they also concentrated on the East coast convoys and ventured along the Sussex cliffs to raid Portland Harbour. The day was also unique in that for the first time, ME 110s provided the escort for a formation of JU 87s instead of the usual 109s. After the morning raid, it was the turn of Tangmere's 601 Squadron to scramble to intercept a force of JU 87s of Luftflotte 3 which were being escorted by ME 110s of Zerstorergeschwader 76 operating from Abbeville and Laval. The size of the enemy armada alarmed 601 who had assumed that it was a single raider. They did however have the advantage of being 'up sun' and they accordingly surprised the enemy by diving and shooting down two Stukas before the German pilots had time to break. They also got four probables and one damaged for no loss to themselves and returned to Tangmere in triumphant mood. They were scrambled again later in the day when a force of HE 111s approached Portsmouth. 601 met them over the Isle of Wight and immediately broke them into two sections, one to attack the bombers and the other the fighters. The enemy force split and although several of the bombers got through and bombed the harbour, six Heinkels were shot down. Hurricane P3681 received bullets in its gravity tank and crashed at Cranmore on the Isle of Wight. The pilot, Sgt. A W Wooley managed to bale out but not before being badly burnt as well as wounded.

In the same raid, 145 Squadron had been scrambled at around the same time as 601. They caught the enemy as they turned for home, and the fight passed over the Sussex coastline to mid Channel. In one ferocious dogfight, Hurricane P2951 was hit in the engine and with glycol streaming from it, F/O G R Branch turned and headed back to Tangmere to land safely and with his aircraft repairable. Not so lucky was Sqn.Ldr J R A Peel in Hurricane P3400 who was shot down in the Channel at 6.25 pm and rescued by the Selsey lifeboat. The Luftwaffe, however, suffered badly in this raid losing 25 aircraft for a total of 168 bombs dropped. One of the more spectacular episodes was the shooting down of Heinkel HE 111H (2648) by two pilots from 145 Squadron, P/O Lord R U P Kay-Shuttleworth and P/O E C J Wakeham. No. 2 Gruppe of KG 55 were attacking the dockyard when 145 arrived on the scene. Diving into the midst of the bomber, the two Hurricanes both shot at the Heinkel which immediately dropped its bombs and began to smoke from the port engine. Realising that he was about to crash, the German pilot put the aircraft down heavily at East Beach, Selsey, where it immediately burst into flames. Seeing the crew leap from the aircraft, a local Army unit approached and captured four of them. Though badly wounded, Oberlt. S Schwein-hagen, Oberfw. E Slotosch, Oberfw. H Schluter and FW. H Steiner offered slight resistance but were overcome and taken to hospital. The last crew member, Uffz. W Muller died in the flames and later Oberfw. Schluter died of his injuries. Both men were buried in St Andrew's churchyard at Tangmere with military honours where they remain to this day. For 145 Squadron it had been quite a day.

The next two days saw more attacks on Portland and by night, minelaying in the Thames Estuary. On the Saturday, 43 Squadron lost two Hurricanes, once again both pilots surviving unhurt. It was the shortage of pilots that worried Dowding and Park, even at this early stage of the war. Before Dunkirk, squadron strengths averaged 17 pilots but the quickening tempo of the war and the constant losses resulted in a smaller number by the time of the real Battle of Britain.

Although Training Command was passing pilots out as quickly as possible, Dowding and Park knew that at the present rate of losses they would soon be in severe trouble. They also knew that when the full brunt of the enemy attacks fell upon the airfields, the losses could only get worse.

The 19th July was to be a bad day for 43 Squadron, who had been roused from their slumber at dawn to be at readiness. The early morning saw showers but as the light slowly increased, bright intervals became apparent. As the morning wore on, the crews got restless with the lack of activity. Some air testing of the Hurricanes was carried out during this quiet period but it was not until around 4 pm that the radar stations warned of a large gathering of enemy aircraft over the Pas-de-Calais. As they crossed the Channel it became obvious they were making for Dover, and just as the sirens wailed in the town, the Luftwaffe appeared overhead. The Heinkel bombers of KG 55 were escorted by the 109s of No. 3 Gruppe of JG 27 operating from Carquebut, and were met initially by Nos. 32, 64 and 74 squadrons. 'A' flight of 43 Squadron and several Hurricanes of 145 were scrambled from Tangmere a short time after the other three squadrons. With a day of no action the scramble could not come soon enough. Meeting the enemy just off the coast, 'A' flight found that their six Hurricanes were up against 12 of the enemy. Both units fell among the returning German aircraft but the pilots of JG 27 were intent on scoring victories. Almost together, three Hurricanes of 43 Squadron came to grief over the Channel. First to fall was Fl/Lt. J W C Simpson whose aircraft was shot down by Oblt. Adolph at around 5.15 pm. He managed to bale out with a bullet in his ankle and his Hurricane crashed in the sea. Drifting over the coastline, FL/Lt. Simpson further injured himself by breaking his collar bone in a heavy landing at West Worthing. Taken to hospital, he was back with his squadron within two weeks.

Around the same time, Hurricane P3468 flown by Sgt. J L Crisp also fell to the guns of JG 27 as did P3531 five minutes later. Whilst Sgt. Crisp lived to fly another day, Sgt. J A Buck, who had also baled out, drowned in the Channel due to the lack of air-sea rescue facilities. His body was recovered from the sea the next day.

The rest of July was spent in similar vein with German attacks on Channel shipping continuing and the Kent coastal towns receiving their first air raids. 145 Squadron moved over to Westhampnett, the satellite airfield, on 23rd July and with 601 now resident at Tangmere in their place, the pace continued. Friday 26th saw 601 lose Hurricane P2753 when a 109 of JG 27 piloted by Oblt. Dobislav shot it down two miles off St Catherine's Point. The pilot, P/O Chaloner Lindsey was never found.

The number of attacks increased as August approached and with high pressure becoming established over Britain, the Luftwaffe made full use of the good weather. Thurday 1st August saw both east and south coast shipping attacked with further minelaying in the Thames estuary and the north east Scottish coast by night. In the German High Command, a directive numbered No. 17 and dated 1st August 1940 from Adolf Hitler made it clear that in order to effect an invasion of Britain in the autumn of 1940, the Luftwaffe was to overpower the RAF in the shortest possible time. It ended by saying, 'the intensification of the air war may begin on or after August 15th'. In fact it had begun some time earlier but from 1st to 7th August, Tangmere was to suffer no losses.

During this period, Fighter Command were flying anything from 200 to 400 sorties a day and as if to reaffirm the directive from Hitler, General Sander, broadcasting to the German people on 7th August, hinted that the tactics of the Luftwaffe were about to change and that the main weapon would be the bomber. What Dowding and Fighter Command feared was about to happen. The heat was to be switched from the shipping to the airfields. The dawn of 'Adler Tag' (Eagle Day) was very near.

On the 8th August 1940, Tangmere had Nos. 43 and 601 still in residence. Fighter Command had 55 squadrons with six under training. Germany had 4,632 aircraft of which 3,306 were serviceable. The odds were very uneven as the two Tangmere squadrons saw action every day. Thursday 8th August marked the beginning of the second stage of the Battle. The weather in the morning was good with visibility six to eight miles and a light cloud cover at 2,000 ft giving good cover for enemy aircraft. The first raid of the day took place at 9 am over a convoy code-named 'Peewit' that was moving through the Channel. The convoy had already been attacked by German 'E' Boats. Now, Stukas of Fliegerkorps VIII escorted by 109s of JG 27 attacked but were successfully chased away by other squadrons in No. 11 Group. 12.45 am brought fresh attacks on the convoy and by the late afternoon, 43 Squadron were scrambled. A giant battle commenced near the Isle of Wight with the enemy being the main loser with 27 aircraft lost and another 18 damaged. 43 Squadron lost six Hurricanes with two pilots lost, P/O J Cruttenden and P/O J R S Delofse.

Monday 12th August saw raids on Portsmouth, convoys in the estuary and the first of many heavy attacks on the radar stations and coastal airfields. With this intensification of the raids, 266 Squadron arrived on the 9th with the first Spitfires to use Tangmere but stayed only three days before moving over to Eastchurch in Kent. On their last day, whilst defending the Portsmouth area and the radar station at Ventnor on the Isle of Wight, they lost two aircraft with one pilot missing.

'Adler Tag' dawned on Tuesday 13th August but was not as the weathermen in Germany had predicted. A cold, damp bank of cloud enclosed the Channel making it virtually impossible to see the water from the air. To the 74 DO 17s of KG 2 based at Cambrai and St Leger, it appeared as though the long awaited assault on the British airfields would have to be postponed. No such message was received and consequently they were airborne by 5.30 am. Led by Oberst. Johannes Fink, they circled the French coast waiting for their fighter escort. Several minutes later the ME 110 fighters emerged from the murky

One that did not get away. A Heinkel 111 downed at High Salvington after a raid on Tangmere (Worthing Gazette).

cloud but did not take up their stations to escort the bombers. Instead they flew straight past Fink and his bombers and began to dive for the ground. Outraged and puzzled by the fighters' actions, Fink could wait no longer and turned to lead his armada over the Channel. What he did not know was that due to the bad weather, this first raid had been aborted but only the fighters had received the recall. Fink, in complete oblivion, proceeded with the operation. His target was the Kent airfield at Eastchurch and the town of Sheerness. (Fink's devastating attack on Eastchurch did not hinder Fighter Command however, because Eastchurch was a Coastal Command airfield.)

By noon, no further raids had been carried out due to the weather and it was plain that the main thrust of the assault had not gone as promised. Some time after midday, the clouds did appear to be breaking but the scheduled attack by bombers of KG 54 was cancelled although the fighter escort of 110s from Zerstorer Group 2 arrived at the rendezvous and, finding no bombers, pressed on for Portland on their own. It was a bad decision for they were met by several squadrons including 601 from Tangmere. For the enemy it proved disastrous as five 110s were instantly shot down. 601 lost four Hurricanes but no pilots and out of the four aircraft, three were repairable.

The really big raids of 'Eagle Day' came later in the afternoon and again one of the targets was Portland. A force of JU 88s from KG 54 and another from LG 1 crossed the Sussex coast and headed for the naval base. In this raid, Southampton was also to receive a bad attack, the first of many to come. The enemy force was met by Hurricanes from both 43 and 601 squadrons and once again, the Luftwaffe were to lose many aircraft. Just three Hurricanes were lost from 43 with the pilots all baling out safely. One aircraft was deemed repairable. The Luftwaffe lost DO 17s, JU 88s, JU 87s, ME 109s and ME 110s, the crews of which had fought very courageously. Again many of them did not survive the battle and when night fell on the 13th, many families in Germany as well as in Britain, were mourning their loved ones. At the end of the day the final loss to Fighter Command was 13 for a total of 700 sorties. For the enemy it was a total of 45 aircraft lost for 1,485 sorties. The exaggeration factor became prominent on this day when the Luftwaffe reported to Hitler that it had destroyed 70 Spitfires and Hurricanes and 18 Blenheims, an error of 700 per cent. In actual fact the first day of the assault had not gone at all well for them.

At Tangmere, 43 and 601 were stood down as night fell. Many very weary pilots took to their local pubs before trying to sleep through a very unsettled night, wondering just what the next day would bring. In the hangars and on the dispersal areas, the groundcrews were toiling to prepare the maximum number of aircraft for the next morning. Refuelling, rearming, repairing damaged airframes, they worked through the entire night stopping only for refreshment and to grab odd minutes of sleep. As the morning of the 14th dawned, a ridge of high pressure promised warm, sunny weather. Tangmere was at readiness at first light but was not called upon until well after midday. After their efforts of the previous day, the Luftwaffe did not put in as many sorties although Dover and the Kentish airfields were attacked during the morning (see *Kent Airfields Remembered*). 43 Squadron were eventually scrambled at 7 pm with Hurricane L1739 piloted by Sgt. H F Montgomery intercepting an HE 111 40 miles south of Beachy Head. From this sortie, he failed to return and was lost at sea. His body was washed ashore in France sometime later and he was buried in Senneville-sur-Fecamp churchyard where he lies today.

The next day, Thursday, saw early reconnaissance flights by the Luftwaffe taking place heralding what was to become later known as 'Black Thursday' for the German High Command. With the ridge of high pressure still dominating the weather over Britain, the Luftwaffe prepared its largest forces so far in the campaign. Every available fighter was to be used plus major divisions of the bomber and dive bomber units. It was the intention of the armada to hit as many radar stations and airfields as possible in the hope that this would bring the British fighters in to battle who then would be swiftly dispatched by the escorting ME 109s and 110s. It did not however, quite work out that way!

The early morning was fairly quiet until 11 am when the first waves were plotted crossing the Channel. Many of the Kentish airfields were hit by this wave and later on, the east coast suffered the first of a series of raids. By noon it was again the turn of Kent and 43 Squadron were scrambled from Tangmere by 12.30 pm. It was just in the nick of time as the JU 87s of SG 2 approached the southern end of their base. Screaming down in a near vertical dive, they released their bombs and Tangmere was enveloped in smoke and flames. One of the hangars was hit, some of the accommodation blocks and five Blenheims of the FIU together with a single Hurricane of 43 Squadron

47

that was unserviceable were destroyed on the ground. As the station personnel not on duty ran for the shelters, 43 Squadron promptly arrived overhead their beloved Tangmere and ploughed into the Stukas, shooting down nine and damaging three more. This was by far the worst defeat of the day for the Germans but it was not without loss to Tangmere. 43 Squadron suffered two Hurricanes damaged and 601 Squadron lost one with another damaged. Despite this the odds were firmly in favour of the RAF, for the total cost to the Luftwaffe of their greatest effort so far in the war was 72 aircraft. British losses were less than half with 34 aircraft lost, 17 pilots killed and 16 wounded. Although this had proved quite a day for Tangmere, the next was to prove disastrous.

Friday the 16th dawned a hot sunny day as clearance from the Stuka raid on Tangmere continued. The grass landing area was still full of craters as all off duty personnel toiled to fill them as best possible. The WAAFs, who until then had been regarded with some doubts as to how they would react under fire, also turned out to help. Those who did not volunteer for filling bomb craters were busy organising field kitchens and first-aid centres for the wounded. At the end of the day no-one could say that they had not remained calm whilst under attack, and indeed their work in all the aftermath of the raid was second to none.

With work continuing all day, a pall of smoke, which seemed not to want to disperse hung over Tangmere. Despite the intense damage, the all-important and vital Sector Operations room was still functional. The morning of the 16th began quietly, allowing the task of clearing up to continue until midday when the first raiders crossed the Kent and Sussex coast. One wave headed for the Thames Estuary, the second for Dover and the third for Portsmouth and Southampton. Once over Portland the force split yet again and sections headed for Ventnor radar station, Tangmere and Gosport. At Ventnor the five Stukas finished off what the previous raids had started and effectively the radar station was out of action until the 23rd August when a mobile unit was established. It was at Tangmere however that the Luftwaffe scored their biggest blow when a force of Stukas approached the airfield at around 1 pm. With clearance still going on, 43 and 601 managed to dodge the craters and get airborne in order to attack the enemy. Some of them however got through and, diving out of the sun, dropped their bombs with great accuracy

A pall of smoke hangs over Tangmere after the crippling raids of 15/16 August 1940.

leaving the airfield in a sorry state. Two of the remaining Belfast hangars (so-named because of the Belfast wooden truss method of supporting the roof) were destroyed together with the station workshops, stores, sick quarters and shelters. The Officers' mess, the Y-Service hut and a Salvation Army hut were all badly damaged but it was the loss of aircraft on the ground together with the loss of life that surprised everyone. Tangmere had never before suffered like this. Six Blenheims, which were the remaining aircraft of the FIU, seven Hurricanes and one Magister were either destroyed or badly damaged. On this occasion there was a tragic loss of life with ten RAF personnel and three civilians killed and another 20 wounded. It was a sad day for all.

As both squadrons returned to Tangmere, they found it difficult to see anything from the air as the smoke continued to billow higher. Somehow they managed to get down and were hastily refuelled and rearmed in preparation for the next scramble. 43 Squadron had suffered badly losing four Hurricanes on the ground and four in the air, luckily with no loss of life. Miraculously, the airfield remained operational throughout the onslaught with just the Sector Operations room having to be relocated in a school in Chichester.

The work of clearance continued day and night and by coincidence 17th August was a quiet day for the Luftwaffe who only carried out a series of reconnaissance flights to judge their previous day's work. Thus the job of reconstruction was able to carry on unhindered. The shortage of pilots was by now a distinct worry to Dowding who eventually persuaded the Air Staff to release some Fairey Battle light bomber pilots from bomber and general reconnaissance squadrons, together with a few Lysander pilots. The situation was becoming desperate.

The 18th August saw the Luftwaffe attempting to finish the airfields in another huge flourish. The faulty German intelligence network had given Goering the impression that the RAF was slowly succumbing to defeat. The first of the raids took place at midday, mainly on Kent airfields, with the second major assault coming in the afternoon on the major Sussex airfields and Poling Radar station. No. 43 were again the first airborne with 601 and 602 following. One of the main targets was Poling Radar between Arundel and Littlehampton. Around 90 bombs were dropped by the Stukas of Stukageschwader 77 operating from Caen who damaged the station so badly that a

Awaiting the call to scramble. Pilots of 43 Squadron kitted for action (A. Saunders Collection).

mobile unit had to be installed to fill the gap in the radar cover. Both 43 and 601 tore into the Stukas with the result that 12 were shot down, these losses determining that the aircraft was not used again in attacks over Britain. So ended a very decisive day. Fighter Command in 766 sorties and together with Ack Ack units, had shot down 71 enemy aircraft for a loss of 27 fighters with ten pilots killed. The results of the German losses made Goering think very hard indeed, for from 15th to 18th August, the Luftwaffe had lost 194 aircraft thus proving that Fighter Command was by no means beaten.

601 were sent for a rest, their place being taken by No. 17 who flew their Hurricanes in from Debden. With the tremendous amount of pressure upon Fighter Command, it was imperative that battle-weary squadrons were withdrawn from the front line stations for rest periods. It also allowed the squadrons from other groups to gain battle experience.

The next few days were cloudy and consequently the Luftwaffe did not carry out the mass raids of the previous days. Monday 26th August was a bad day for 43 Squadron as raids over Portsmouth and the Solent developed. Around 4.45 pm, they engaged the enemy over the city and lost six Hurricanes but all the pilots survived though they were injured.

The raids continued for the rest of the month but Tangmere did not have another large raid until the 30th. Fair weather had returned and the Luftwaffe again mounted the first of several big raids. The morning saw Kent airfields attacked but at 1.30 pm a large force of Heinkels and Junkers headed for Biggin Hill, Shoreham and Tangmere. With 43 and 17 Squadrons airborne over Kent, the airfield received another large blow as the work of the previous reconstruction was once again ruined. It was another black day for 43 Squadron as their Commanding Officer, Squadron Leader 'Tubby' Badger, was shot down and very badly injured. He survived his injuries for nine months before the pain and trauma proved too much. Also lost was Sergeant Noble, and it was a very sad squadron that landed back at a partly demolished Tangmere.

The 31st saw Fighter Command's heaviest losses with 39 aircraft shot down and 14 pilots lost. Although 43 and 17 were in action, they lost no aircraft on this day but of notable worry to Dowding at this crucial stage of the Battle was the fatigue rate and the rising toll of pilots killed. Several of the major airfields including Tangmere had been bombed and were barely operational. The coastal Radar chain had been severely hit with several sites only just operating. This was not of course known to the German Intelligence Service due to the effectiveness of some of the mobile units quickly brought in to 'patch' a hole in the chain. It was however, a harrowing time and all the signs were that the punishment would continue.

September came in with a spell of fine weather as 601 returned to Tangmere. Somewhat refreshed, the fighting partnership of 43 and 601 once again got underway but for a limited period only as the latter were posted to Exeter after only five days at the airfield. Their replacement, No. 213, flew up from Exeter the same day and had settled in by nightfall.

The fourth phase of the Battle is deemed to have started on 7th September 1940. The timetable for the invasion of Britain was not going at all well, for far from diminishing, the RAF appeared to be gathering strength in the air. Unbeknown to Goering and the German intelligence, reinforcements were being brought in from all the other groups in the UK thus creating the impression that the RAF were indeed gaining superiority. For some time however, some of the Luftwaffe commanders had been of the impression that a quick defeat of the British nation must involve bombing its heart, London. An

The Spitfire of Douglas Bader, when he commanded Tangmere wing in early 1941, seen here over Beachy Head. From a painting by Colin Doggett.

accident during August had involved several German aircraft dropping bombs on London (a case of bad navigation). The RAF immediately retaliated with sorties over Berlin and this decided both Hitler and Goering to change tactics. This fourth phase took the heat from the airfields at the expense of London and its people.

Although the attacks on the airfields became less, the squadrons continued to fight against overwhelming odds. Sunday 8th September saw 43 Squadron lose Hurricane L1727 but worse was to come the next day when 607 (County of Durham) Squadron, Royal Auxiliary Air Force, who had arrived at Tangmere on 1st September, lost no less than six Hurricanes with three of the pilots killed.

The fight continued throughout September and on the 14th, Hitler decided to postpone 'Sealion', the planned invasion of England. He blamed the weather for lack of air superiority but was still assured that by the 17th, the new date set for 'Sealion', the way would be clear. The 15th September, now celebrated annually as Battle of Britain day, saw very heavy fighting with large attacks on London.

It fell on a Sunday and by 11 am, just as people were going to church, mass formations were plotted forming up over Boulogne and Calais. Both 10 and 12 Groups came to the assistance of No. 11 and both the Tangmere squadrons gave a good account of themselves with just one Hurricane lost from 607 Squadron, Pilot Officer Stephenson baling out and surviving.

The Germans had expected great things of this day but it was not to be, with losses the highest since 18th August. Once again 'Sealion' was postponed but the German build-up of barges in the French Channel ports continued. The threat was still very real as Tangmere, now home to 213 and 607 Squadron since 43 had departed to Usworth on 8th September, continued its war.

In order to confuse the enemy, a dummy airfield for Tangmere was set up at Gumber as the Battle entered its fifth and final stage. With losses of 1,653 aircraft, the Luftwaffe had still not gained superiority and with as many air-raids by night as well as by day, Hitler could not understand why England had not fallen. October began with some more raids upon 11 Group airfields but still the main target was

Pilots Will E Gore and Mike Irving snatch a few hours rest between sorties (W. Blackadder DSO).

54

London and the principal cities. 607 lost several Hurricanes on 5th October but after five weeks at Tangmere left for Turnhouse on the 10th, being replaced by a jubilant No. 145, glad to be back in the front line once again.

The rest of the month saw 145 and 213 fighting side by side until, with dark nights and changeable weather setting in, by early November the Battle of Britain was deemed to be over. The pressure still continued on Fighter Command but with Hitler postponing 'Sealion' until possibly early 1941, the main thrust of the German attacks came by night. The Blitz proper had begun.

The Fighter Command Order of Battle for 3rd November 1940 stated that Tangmere had 145 and 213 Squadrons with Hurricanes resident. With the changing season, the Luftwaffe clearly knew it was impossible to remedy the situation of non-dominance in the air. Thus the extreme heat was cooling a little for the airfields as 213 Squadron left Tangmere for Leconfield on 29th November. Back to Tangmere came 145 to continue the fight. The first Bristol Beaufighters to use the airfield had arrived on 12th October when a detachment from 219 Squadron flew in from Redhill. The Beaufighter had added a new concept to the RAF for it was the first night-fighter to use AI (Airborne Interception) Radar against the nightly raids. It was both a fast and heavily armed aircraft and 219 were the first squadron to receive the AI equipped aircraft. With the Beaufighter, Fighter Command had the capability to defend the UK by night.

To accompany 145 Squadron in the day defence rôle came the Spitfires of No. 65 (East India) Squadron and it was with these units that Tangmere celebrated Christmas. Unlike 1939, the season had a feeling of uncertainty about it and the squadrons were kept active throughout the period. This was the beginning of a new phase of attacks, for although the pressure had eased for the airfields, the freedom of the German bombers to roam over the cities at night was an appalling burden for the public to bear.

The New Year saw a change as 145 and 65 Squadrons exchanged their Hurricanes for Spitfires. The rest of 219 Squadron had arrived at Tangmere from Redhill and were carrying out regular night sorties, enjoying a certain amount of success. On 13th March 1941 a force of bombers flew in low over the coast and attacked Tangmere, the first raid in some considerable time. With the majority of the country covered in fog, Tangmere on the coast was one of the few stations operating that night. Bombing raids had been carried out over enemy territory and the returning aircraft were advised to use the south east airfields including Tangmere to land. At about the same time that some of the bombers were landing at the airfield, a force of enemy aircraft appeared over it and commenced to drop their bombs. 219 were already airborne and under the control of Wartling Radar, one of the many Ground Controlled Interception Radars that had begun operating to assist the night-fighters in finding the enemy aircraft. They were given a course to steer by the Radar Controller which brought them to within striking distance of the enemy, whereupon the aircrafts' own AI radar picked them up. In two separate attacks, 219 shot down four of the enemy bombers that had been attacking Tangmere. On the ground, the landing area was once again partially cratered but with just one barrack block destroyed and no casualties, the airfield suffered very little.

Clear moonlight nights would see the Beaufighters roaming over Kent and Sussex looking for 'trade'. With large scale daylight raids a thing of the past, there was plenty of it for the night-fighter crews. It could be very frustrating for them however as the AI radar sets they carried were sometimes very unreliable. Ground echoes gave a false reading to the navigator and sometimes the echo or 'blip' just faded altogether. It was then back to either relying on the GCI radar controller to find the enemy or to one's own eyesight.

65 Squadron were posted to Kirton-on-Lindsey in February to be replaced by 616 (South Yorkshire) Squadron of the Royal Auxiliary Air Force. The Spitfire Squadrons, now collectively known as the 'Tangmere Wing' began offensive sweeps across the Channel and Northern France, harassing as much as possible. This new type of operation, known as 'Rodeos' was intended to cause as much confusion and damage to the enemy as the previous months had caused to Fighter Command. After a year of being very much on the defensive, the RAF were now able to carry the war back to the enemy.

In May 1941 both Spitfire squadrons moved to Westhampnett, the satellite, to continue the day operations, whilst in March a detachment of 23 Squadron flew in from Ford, just two minutes flying time away. The squadron flew the Douglas Havoc, also known as Boston, which was an American built aircraft that had been used by the French Air Force before they were overrun by the enemy. The balance of the French consignment was taken over by the RAF and

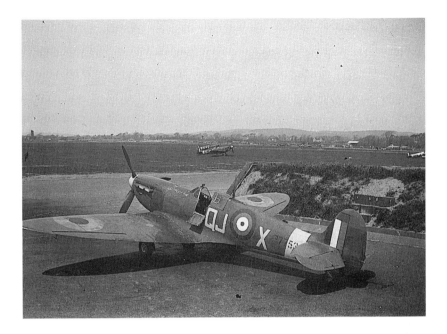

'Buck' Casson's Spitfire pictured at Tangmere shortly before it was lost in a dogfight in May 1941 (A. Saunders Collection).

converted for night-fighting. The Havoc was a twin engined aircraft of all metal stressed skin construction, armed with eight 303 Browning machine guns firing forward and one Vickers 'K' gun mounted in the rear cockpit. 23 Squadron used the Havoc for night intrusion operations over France and together with the Beaufighters of 219 Squadron, the name of Tangmere became synonymous with night-fighting.

Although not normally associated with clandestine operations, the airfield during the summer of 1941 became just that when Westland Lysanders of the SOE landed to pick up agents, who were temporarily accommodated in Tangmere Cottage, a picturesque little house just across the road. Belonging to the Special Duty Squadrons, the Lysanders were normally painted entirely black with no squadron or serial number markings. These operations were first carried out in 1940 but from the spring of 1941 the aircraft were regular visitors to Tangmere.

*A defiant gesture from the CO of No. 1 Squadron, Squadron Leader J A F Maclachlan
– 'One-armed Mac' (No. 1 Squadron).*

On 1st July, No. 1 Squadron returned albeit for a brief period. Flying Hurricane IIBs, they were used in the nightfighter role, but not in the conventional way, for they flew in company with a squadron known as the 'Turbinlite' unit. In the case of Tangmere it was 1455 Flight who were equipped once again with the Douglas Havoc, but this time their aircraft were fitted with an enormous searchlight in the nose. Hence the name 'Turbinlite'. The idea was that the Havoc would illuminate the enemy aircraft with this great light to enable the formating Hurricanes to shoot it down. It proved a very unsatisfactory way of dealing with enemy aircraft at night and many good crews were lost during the 'Turbinlite' operations until the units were disbanded at the end of 1941.

With so many operations now taking place across the Channel, a detachment of 277 Squadron was formed at Tangmere, borrowing some Lysanders from the Army Co-operations units to use in the Air Sea Rescue role. Though not the ideal aircraft for this purpose, they served the requirements well and with the facility of being able to attach four dinghies to the wheel spats, many pilots had cause to be grateful to the 'Lizzies'.

During late 1941, further building was carried out at the airfield to repair much of the damage done during the Battle of Britain raids and at the same time it was extended. Included in this update were the construction of two hard runways, the demolition of the one remaining badly damaged hangar, and the construction of several Blister hangars in its place. By July 1941, No. 1 Squadron had converted to the Hurricane IIC, basically the same as the IIB but with the installation of four 20 mm machine guns. 23 and 219 were still active in the night-fighter role, but the end was in sight for the 'Turbinlite' Squadron as No. 1 with their Hurricanes carried out many night patrols alone and without the aid of the Havoc's searchlight.

Although it had been intended that No. 1 Squadron should go elsewhere, they stayed the winter at Tangmere, continuing night patrols with limited success. Christmas 1941 came and went and although the war was now being carried back to the enemy, the longed-for end of hostilities seemed far off.

1942 saw changes at Tangmere and No. 1 finally left for Acklington in July. The 23 Squadron detachment had converted to Mosquitos and departed to Manston, and June saw the Beaufighters of 219 also posted to Acklington. 277 ASR had acquired a Walrus amphibian aircraft to replace the largely unsuitable Lysanders and in July they further converted to Boulton Paul Defiants. Tangmere was not left empty for long as the Hurricane IICs of 43 Squadron flew in from Acklington. The 'Fighting Cocks' were back.

Wednesday 19th August 1942 is the day that people should never forget. In the early hours of this fateful day, more than 6,000 men were landed in France determined to create a knock-out blow to Hitler's troops stationed there. The operation was code-named 'Jubilee' but is more commonly known as the Dieppe raid. It was on this day that the Canadian Army lost more men, captured as prisoners of war, than they did anywhere else.

For some time Tangmere had abounded with rumours of an impending operation. It was known that it was to be a day offensive and the departure of the night-fighters was a further indication of the type of operation. From 12th August, Tangmere was subject to intense security as meetings were held behind closed doors, guarded by armed military police. The arrival of 41 Squadron and their Spitfire

VBs from Llanbedr heralded the beginning of a hectic week for the airfield. On 20th August, No. 66 joined Nos. 118 and 501 at Tangmere, all three squadrons joining together to form the Ibsley wing of Spitfires. The stage was set!

At first light on the 19th, the Hurricanes of 43 were airborne to join with other squadrons operating from Shoreham, just along the coast from Tangmere. They carried out attacks on gun positions near Dieppe but were themselves shot at by the ground defences, losing two aircraft. On their return to Tangmere, No. 41's Spitfires took over to escort Canadian Squadron No. 412 who were operating from Merston, another satellite airfield to Tangmere. These operations continued throughout the day with squadrons landing, refuelling and rearming, then going back to the fray. By nightfall on this fateful day, Tangmere squadrons had flown over 400 sorties with success but the spirits of the pilots were low as they had all witnessed the slaughter below.

With 'Jubilee' over, the airfield resorted to carrying on the offensive operations over Europe and many Spitfire squadrons used the airfield for short periods. In addition to the routine 'Rhubarb' sorties were added 'Ramrods', so called because they were daylight escorts to bombing raids. One of the more unusual squadrons to be based at Tangmere was No. 823 of the Fleet Air Arm who operated the Fairey Albacore Torpedo carrying aircraft to attack enemy shipping in the Straits. It became obvious that rivalry would spring up between the fighter pilots and the naval aviators stationed on the same airfield, but the punishment that the Albacore pilots suffered at the hands of the enemy guns ensured them the great respect of their fellow pilots.

The first Hawker Typhoons to operate from Tangmere arrived with 486 (Royal New Zealand Air Force) Squadron when they flew in from West Malling on 29th October 1942. A new breed of fighter, the Typhoon got off to a bad start in the RAF for it failed in the role of an interceptor fighter. It did however go on to achieve fame as a close support aircraft carrying out hit and run raids over enemy territory. Despite this, 486 did achieve success using the aircraft in the fighter role, and December was a very good month for the Squadron.

Christmas 1942 was a busy period as a new type of operation called 'Roadsteds', attacks against enemy shipping, got underway. The Typhoon was the ideal aircraft for this type of warfare, so much so that by March 1943, 486 had been joined by 83 Squadron and 197

60

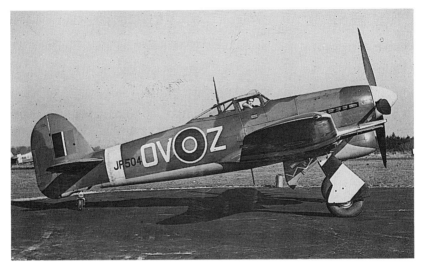

The Hawker Typhoons of 197 Squadron arrived at Tangmere on the 28th March 1943 to carry out fighter patrols and bomber escort missions. Pictured in his Typhoon IB is the CO Sqd. Ldr M C Holmes DFC (Imperial War Museum).

Squadron, all flying Typhoons. With three squadrons stationed at Tangmere, the noise from the Sabre engines became intolerable to the local inhabitants. Another drawback to this engine was the starting problem and in order to overcome this, the Typhoons were run-up at all hours of the night and day. Apart from the noise upsetting the public, many groundcrew members cursed as they struggled from their warm beds in winter in order to run the engines up. With them it was not a popular aircraft!

With the war now clearly going in the Allies' favour, the offensive operations across the Channel increased. 486 were carrying 500 lb bombs to harass enemy shipping and French, Belgian and Dutch harbours were strafed with gun fire. The other two units continued flying 'Rhubarbs and Ramrods'. 197, led by the CO, Squadron Leader M C Homes DFC, enjoyed a particularly good period at Tangmere and achieved a lot of success during 'Operation Starkey', the feint (a 'sham' attack to divert attention from the main attack) and large scale operation over the Pas-de-Calais in September.

Spitfires returned to Tangmere in October in the form of Nos. 41 and 91 (Nigeria) Squadrons as they flew in from the satellite at Westhampnett. They immediately commenced 'Rodeo' sweeps across enemy territory and claimed nine enemy aircraft for no loss on 20th October when they were attacked by a superior force of FW 190s and ME 109s.

With Tangmere being on the coast, it was obvious that it would be one of the first airfields that many of the returning bombers would see. From 1943, it became an emergency airfield for such aircraft returning in distress, and mornings would often find British and American bombers sitting around the perimeter with various degrees of damage. They were hastily patched up by the groundcrews until considered airworthy whereupon they would leave for their own bases. This situation continued well into 1944, many pilots blessing the fact that Tangmere was there.

Towards the end of the year the Spitfires began escorting American bombers to the V1 rocket sites in France whilst the Typhoons continued their offensive operations. The clandestine sorties were still being flown from Tangmere with a detachment of 161 Squadron, still with Lysanders. One of the more memorable episodes of this type of warfare concerned a Lysander flown by Flying Officer McCairns. Departing from Tangmere, he approached the agreed field in France to see torches burning in a field about two miles away. The Resistance were in the wrong field and giving the wrong code signal. But what should F/O McCairns do! It could well be the Gestapo giving false messages, it could be anything. He decided to put down at the further torch lit field and have a look. As he landed, figures came rushing out of the woods. Frenchmen! Why had they not kept to the agreed field? Why the wrong signal? 'Ah Monsieur. This was a much better field and a simple mistake with the signal.' It was all very confusing for F/O McCairns. As if that was not enough, he was asked to take four strapping heavy Frenchmen back to England. How the little Lysander ever got airborne was a miracle, no less the landing back at Tangmere. Such were the sorties of the SOE!

The New Year of 1944 saw the Typhoons of 197 and 486 and the Spitfires XIIs of 41 and 91 in residence. The black painted Lysanders were still apparent but it was the whisper of an Allied invasion in 1944 that was on everyone's lips. As if in preparation for this event, No. 84 Typhoon Wing formed at Tangmere and became known as 146 Airfield. This required the addition of Nos. 183 and 257 Typhoon squadrons who flew in from Predannack and Beaulieu respectively.

The wing was commanded by Wing Commander D E Gillan DSO, DFC and Bar who led many very successful raids on the V1 sites in Northern France. By 16th March, Nos. 183 and 197 had left Tangmere and were in turn replaced by 198 and 609 (West Riding) Squadrons, both flying Typhoons, to carry on the offensive operations over Europe. Now armed with rockets, the aircraft carried out devastating attacks on enemy communications, coastal defence works and radar stations. All of this was in preparation for the long awaited Allied invasion of Europe which would herald the beginning of the end of the Third Reich. They stayed but a week and then left to form part of the 2nd Tactical Air Force. In their place came 266 (Rhodesia) Squadron bringing their Typhoons down from Acklington. They stayed a little longer but with the plans for the invasion well advanced, squadrons came and went from Tangmere within weeks.

It was now the turn of the Spitfires as 126 and 127 Airfields of the Royal Canadian Air Force took over Tangmere. Nos. 401, 411 and 412 arrived from Biggin Hill followed by 403, 416 and 421 from Kenley. They began 'Ranger' operations, deep penetration flights over enemy territory attacking anything that moved. Trains, coaches, cars, they all fell to the guns of the Canadian Spitfires. 416 (City of Oshawa) became the scourge of enemy trains when on 22nd May 1944, they destroyed four trains before turning their attention on a gaggle of FW 190s, downing five into the bargain.

On 6th June 1944 in the greatest combined operation of all time, the Allies landed in France and secured a foothold. American and British troops were landed by airborne and seaborne craft and although suffering many casualties, the assault was the first rush towards Berlin and defeat for Hitler and his army. From dawn on the 6th the Canadians' Spitfires carried out standing patrols over the beachheads and further inland, clashing with FW 190s and ME 109s. By 18th June, the Canadians had flown to temporary airfields in France, and Tangmere became home to 66 Squadron, together with 331 and 332 Norwegian Squadrons flying the Spitfire IX. They arrived in the morning of 22nd June and by the afternoon they had been joined by a Czech wing comprising Nos. 310, 312 and 313 Squadrons. It was a very busy time for Tangmere with many units coming and going at regular intervals. Over this hectic period the airfield also saw the Lympne wing arrive, comprising Nos. 33, 74 (Tiger) and 127 Squadrons. At the end of the month the airfield was honoured to receive

Tangmere falls to the vandals. The historic airfield as it was in the 1970s, before the establishment of the Aviation Museum (Portsmouth Publishing and Printing).

a visit from the King and Queen who witnessed 132 Wing departing on an escort mission but did not allow their presence to stop Tangmere operating as normal. After royalty it was the turn of Winston Churchill and later Dwight Eisenhower to visit, but as the Norwegian and Czech wing moved across the Channel, Nos. 222, 349 and 485 arrived for a week before they too went to France.

By September 1944 it was strangely quiet at Tangmere. After the hectic period of the invasion months, the Second Front was now across the Channel and the south coast airfields had lost their strategic position. Christmas 1944 saw a new spirit emerging as people began to realise that the end of the war was in sight.

1945 saw little use of Tangmere. The reformed Central Fighter Establishment began to use the airfield and was the only operational unit to celebrate victory there. Suddenly it was all over but Tangmere was earmarked to play an important role in the peacetime Air Force and a period of expansion and reconstruction began. To replace the hangars that were bombed in the Battle came three T2 (Transportable) sheds and a new surface for the 1,800 yards NE/SW runway. The airfield was also extended southwards and westwards in preparation for the new generation of jet aircraft. New concrete blast walls were erected at the aircraft dispersal areas to deaden the sound of the engines but sadly this reconstruction programme entailed the demolition of the Tangmere Arms, a public house beloved by all the airmen at Tangmere. Doubtless there were very many others in the area to serve their needs!

Tangmere remained operational until 1967, after which it rapidly fell into disrepair and vandalism was rife. Today only the shell of the control tower remains, standing like a forlorn sentinel. The villagers could not let the airfield just slide into obscurity and so erected a memorial stone on the green which was unveiled by the late Group Captain Bader CBE, DSO, DFC on 18th December 1976. A band of dedicated enthusiasts established the Tangmere Military Aviation Museum adjacent to the airfield and this today is one of the main attractions within the area. These two vivid memorials are all that remain of the Sector station of Sector A, Tangmere. It was an airfield with a large part of our history taking place upon its grass, and one which will certainly never be forgotten.

3
FORD

After its use in World War One Ford first reverted to agriculture then was developed by civil aircraft companies (see Chapter One), until the rumblings from Germany became too ominous and the airfield was requisitioned.

It had been acquired by the Air Ministry under the RAF Expansion scheme with the 1938 air estimates including an allocation of £109,000 for a hutted camp and further hangars. These were to be built to house the School of Naval Co-operation which ultimately was to form at Ford. The new buildings were concentrated on the eastern perimeter of the airfield and were standard Air Ministry huts with Bellman hangars. After the School of Naval Co-operation and the Fleet Air Arm transferred to the Admiralty in January 1939, Ford was commissioned as HMS Peregrine. Nos. 750, 751 and 752 Squadrons were formed a few months later out of the RN Observers' School. Equipped with a variety of aircraft such as Sharks and Ospreys and even the Walrus, these ancient aircraft were often to be seen plodding along the Sussex coastline.

On the outbreak of war the school also flew Percival Proctors in the training role. A delightful little aircraft, it was the military version of the Vega Gull light aircraft and was to do sterling work with the Observers' school. The Navy still shared the airfield with Flight Refuelling Ltd from whom the airfield had been requisitioned, and who now occupied the western side of Ford. The two units got on very well but some time later the company moved to Cheltenham to carry on their experimental work. Ford's connection with Sir Alan Cobham, the founder of Flight Refuelling, had gone for ever.

During the 'Phoney War', the Navy carried on with its training routines. The airfield had not been earmarked for expansion to a fighter base and the training units continued their vital role in providing observers and navigators for the operational squadrons aboard the carriers. As June approached and the convoy attacks in the Channel increased, the seamen at Ford could hear the guns of the coastal batteries open up and, on a clear day, see the German bombers, mainly Stukas, diving on the convoys. Hurricanes and Spitfires from neighbouring airfields were heard and seen flying overhead going to the defence of the merchant ships. With July came the opening phase of the Battle and the Sussex sky was often streaked with the tell-tale signs of dogfights. During the past two months, German activity had increased over the Channel and was about to break into the greatest aerial battle ever. Not one of the Fighter Command airfields would be left unscathed and neither, did it seem, would any of the Navy airfields. Ford was to be no exception.

Sunday 18th August dawned fine and fairly warm for this final flourish of the Luftwaffe to destroy Fighter Command in one week. With the main morning raids concentrating on the Kent airfields, it was past noon when it became the turn of the Sussex airfields to be hit. Luftflotte 3 concentrated on airfields and a radar station in the Hampshire/West Sussex area. The impact of the bombing was disastrous as the 28 Stukas of the 2nd Gruppe of StG 77 commenced to annihilate Ford. Operating from Caen and led by Major Chemens Graff von Schonborn, they approached the airfield in line astern. On the ground the seamen and Wrens looked up at the approaching formation, undecided whether or not to run for cover. At first it was suggested by some that they were British fighters but the sight of the Balkan crosses on the wings and the howling of the engines as the aircraft commenced their dive soon changed the onlookers' minds. With a cry of 'take cover', they scurried to the nearest shelters as the Stukas loomed ever nearer.

It was the finale to a day of ever increasing alerts. Since early morning the siren had sounded and the trainee observers from the school had to stop what they were doing and run to the station armoury. Their orders were to draw Vickers machine guns and mount them on the Bedford trucks which were used for airfield defence in states of alert. The constant wailing of the sirens only to be replaced minutes later by the 'all clear' had caused them much consternation, as they had to fit the guns to the trucks several times that morning. The last 'all clear' was still in operation at 2 pm and the gun crews retired to the mess for a well earned lunch. At 2.20 pm there was no change as they left the hall but in the air, the Stuka formation could see the Isle of Wight and Selsey Bill through the thin haze. Below them the Channel was a little choppy as the wind increased but with the haze persisting, the leader of the formation, Helmut Bode, knew that the attack would take the ground defences by surprise. This was the way he wanted it, and a few minutes later part of the force split to head for Gosport. A further five minutes flying time and another group split and headed for Thorney Island leaving 2 Gruppes to deal with Poling radar station and Ford.

Appearing out of the haze the aircraft had the airfield practically to themselves for Ford, not being a fighter airfield, had little defence. Six Lewis guns, the entire permanent airfield defence, began blazing away at the aircraft with little effect. The Stukas bombed with great precision and within seconds, direct hits were scored on fuel installations, MT and store sheds, several messes and two hangars. As the observers ran to the armoury once again to draw their Vickers guns

In August 1940 Ford ('HMS Peregrine') came under such devastating attack by Junkers 87 Stukas that the airfield had to be relinquished by the Admiralty.

a bomb landed beside the building and blew a good portion of it away. By far the worst hit was on the fuel dumps which caught fire instantly with a sheet of flame reaching high into the air. Then came the black smoke which blocked out the daylight and seemed to hang around for hours. As the enemy turned for home they were attacked by 43 Squadron from Tangmere and 145 from Westhampnett who managed to shoot down three between them as the Stukas crossed the coastline. All of this however came too late to save Ford from devastation.

As normality returned, the men and women emerged from the shelters to take stock of the situation. It was utter devastation with five Blackburn Sharks, five Fairey Swordfish, two Fairey Albacores and a Percival Proctor blazing away. Thirteen aircraft in all were lost with a further 26 damaged. By far the worst shock was the loss of life, 28 killed and 75 badly injured with many more suffering slight injuries from flying debris. There were also several acts of courage and defiance. One of the bombs had exploded next to a shelter in which around 20 seamen and several Wrens had been sheltering. Being so close, the explosion had lifted the top of the shelter off and consequently many of the people inside had been killed by flying shrapnel. One of the Wrens, although injured herself, began to

The Junkers 87 Stuka – aircraft which destroyed 'HMS Peregrine' airfield in August 1940.

administer first aid to the injured with complete disregard for her own safety and had it not been for her prompt action, several others may also have died. One of the acts of defiance came when a naval officer rushed outside from the comparative safety of a building and began to fire his revolver at the diving Stukas. It was a fruitless gesture that cost him his life but such was his rage at the invasion of his airfield by the Germans.

Ten minutes after the Germans had first been sighted approaching the airfield, it was all over. An unreal silence settled over the area as the fuel dump continued pouring its black smoke into the atmosphere. In an effort to put out the raging fires, the local brigade rushed to the airfield and fought side by side with the Naval Fire Service. The police and a fleet of ambulances had also converged on Ford to assist the Naval medical staff with the dead and injured. The former were removed to the village hall in Ford to await the funeral vans and the injured were taken to hospitals in Arundel and Chichester. As darkness fell, the seamen were still toiling to clear the rubble and attempting to get the station back together. It was a fruitless attempt for Ford never fully recovered until much later. 829 Squadron were posted away, part of the Observers' School was transferred to Arbroath in Scotland and part to Trinidad in the West Indies. The detachment left behind by Flight Refuelling Ltd also went back to Cheltenham to join the main company and Ford was left with just a Naval care and maintenance party on site.

By September 1940 with the Battle of Britain still raging overhead, it had been decided that the airfield should be relinquished by the Navy and on the 30th HMS Peregrine was temporarily lost to the history books. Prior to this, on the 12th, No. 23 Squadron had brought their Bristol Blenheim 1Fs down from Wittering, indicating that Ford was about to be enveloped within No. 11 Group of Fighter Command. 23 Squadron soon settled into their new station and quickly took over the accommodation so recently vacated by the Navy. The construction gangs had moved in to repair much of the damage caused by the 18th August raid and by the end of September, some return to normal activities was apparent.

Still a grass airfield, Ford's landing area was quickly patched up by the contractors to allow the Blenheims to begin operations. The 1F was primarily the night-fighter version of the type although 200 were converted from bombers with a conversion kit (consisting of panels,

70

extra armament, etc.) supplied by the Southern Railway Ashford Train Depot. The aircraft had its forward armament with an additional gun pack containing four Browning machine guns under the fuselage. Although it had been specified as a twin-engined day fighter, the Blenheim did not come up to expectations in this role and was hastily fitted with what were called 'magic mirrors' to enable the pilot and observer to see at night. They were of course the forerunners of radar, and in experiments in this new night warfare the Blenheim was to prove itself. 23 Squadron at Ford were fitted with such devices shortly after their arrival. The equipment consisted of a radio transmitter, receiver and the necessary aerials. With the nose aerial sending out pulses, the echo from another aircraft was received on a cathode ray tube in the observer's position. In order to perfect the system, many long hours were flown at night by the men of 23 Squadron culminating in the first ever night intruder sortie being flown by the squadron on the night of 21st/22nd December 1940.

Christmas was celebrated at Ford in the usual style and in common with the majority of airfields in No. 11 Group, the thick snow severely hampered operations over this period. Being a grass airfield Ford was almost unusable in the snow and later the slush. For a blossoming night-fighter station, this was obviously unacceptable and plans were put forward for tarmac runways to be laid.

The New Year saw the FIU move in from Shoreham, just along the coast. It was tasked with developing operational techniques for radar-equipped night-fighter aircraft and had a complement of about 20 officers and 200 men. The aircraft were mainly Blenheims but the FIU also had several of the new Bristol Beaufighters. This was the successor to the Blenheim and was the first night-fighter with a sufficiently high performance to really do combat with the Germans. 23 Squadron were still struggling on with the slower Blenheim but in March 1941 they converted to the Douglas Havoc. Modification of the Bostons to Havocs was carried out at the Burtonwood Aircraft Repair Depot near Liverpool and the aircraft was really a stop-gap night-fighter between the Blenheim and the newer Beaufighters and Mosquitos.

23 Squadron were unique in converting to this aircraft due to the fact that they received the three seat fighter/bomber version known as the 'Moonfighter'. With the squadron specialising in night intrusion over France, the aircraft were also painted in an overall matt

71

With the suggestion of a Victory Roll a Blenheim flies over the wreckage of a Junkers 52 (MAP).

black finish and flame damper exhausts to avoid detection. Detachments of 23 Squadron were sent from Ford to Manston, Tangmere, Bradwell Bay and Middle Wallop and the squadron roamed far afield at night over Holland and France, achieving great success.

The long awaited tarmac runways materialised during spring 1941 when one of 6,000 ft was laid SW/NE and a smaller 4,800 ft laid NW/SE. In addition, a tarmac perimeter track and several hardstandings for aircraft dispersal were built together with a number of Blister hangars and blast pens for aircraft protection. The reconstruction of Ford after the devastating raid of 1940 was nearly complete.

Autumn 1941 saw the FIU continuing their experimental work into newer and better marks of airborne radar. 23 were still flying their night intrusions over German occupied Europe with their Havocs. With the war suddenly escalating into a global conflict after Hitler's invasion of Russia and the attack on Pearl Harbour, a new hardened attitude to get on with the war and finish it became obvious. Progress had already been made in the art of night-fighting as illustrated by the fact that in January 1941, three enemy aircraft were shot down by this method of airborne radar. In May it had become 96! Although there was still a long way to go, the enemy were not now having it all their own way.

The New Year of 1942 still saw the same two units in residence. Although on the home front it seemed as though the war was going relatively well, events around the world were not so good. On 15th February 1941, Singapore surrendered to the Japanese and closer home, Rommel attacked Libya. Not one of these events really had any effect on the operational routine of Ford and it was not until late May when something of a change occurred.

'Operation Jubilee' was planned to mark the beginning of Allied troops landing back on to the European mainland, but it failed miserably. The RAF was to play its part in the Dieppe raid and a change of aircraft took place for 23 Squadron in preparation for 'Jubilee'. They converted from the Havoc to the Douglas Boston as their main rôle changed from night intrusion to day intrusion. Very similar to the Havoc, the Boston was first in action against land targets on 12th February 1942, 88 Squadron making a memorable attack on the Matford works at Poissy on 8th March. The rôle of 23 Squadron was to attack targets in and around the designated landing area at Dieppe. They were joined on 7th June by a reformed 605 (County of Warwick) Squadron which had previously disbanded at Takali, Malta in February 1942. They took over the Bostons and Havocs of 23 Squadron and flew their first operation on 14th July over enemy occupied France. 23 had meanwhile once again undertaken a conversion to the De Havilland Mosquito II and had returned to night intrusion.

The Mk II Mosquito was the fighter version of the three Mosquito prototypes to fly. Indeed the first deliveries of the new and secret night-fighter were made to 23 Squadron at Ford and by July they had entirely replaced the Havocs and Bostons. The Mosquito carried the then highly secret AI Mk. IV and it was hoped that this would result in more of the enemy being shot down at night than ever before. By 6th August however, the squadron had moved to Manston and Ford was left with the FIU and 605 Squadron still flying the Havocs and Bostons.

Earlier in the year the two units had been joined by a detachment of No. 88 (Hong Kong) Squadron who arrived with Boston IIIs and also a detachment of 107 Squadron flying the same type. For a relatively small airfield, Ford was becoming very congested and it became obvious to all, including the local residents, that something big was brewing. By 16th August a veil of secrecy had been thrown around Ford. All was ready for Wednesday 19th August 1942.

Across the other side of the airfield, the FIU were continuing their testing and experimental work of interception equipment. In June 1942 the unit got a new CO, Wing Commander Roderick Chisholm CBE, DSO, DFC. He found a greatly expanded unit comprising about 20 officers and 200 men flying a variety of aircraft including Beaufighters and Mosquitos. By 1942, the enemy had changed his tactics of attack preferring now to fly in fast and low, and to maintain regular evasive actions. To counteract this, the Mosquito was rapidly succeeding the Beaufighter in the night-fighter rôle, and with improved AI and a ground control system to guide the aircraft to within a stone's throw from its quarry, thus allowing the airborne radar to take over, the war was beginning to go our way. Undeterred by the amount of Bostons on the airfield, the FIU under the leadership of Roderick Chisholm continued their test flying throughout the period of 'Jubilee'.

The Beaufighters of No. 141 Squadron flew the short hop from Tangmere to Ford on 10th August 1942 to take part in the operations and as dawn broke on the 19th, the Boston aircrews woke early to undertake the first missions. Four from 88 and four from 107 Squadrons were airborne at first light equipped with smoke bombs to drop between the designated landing beach and the ships approaching that beach-head. Several minutes later further Bostons from Nos. 88, 107, 418 and 605 Squadrons took off to bomb gun emplacements around the Dieppe area. A lot of flak and anti-aircraft fire was unleashed by the Germans at the aircraft resulting in the loss of several Bostons. Immediately their bombs had been dropped, the aircraft turned for home and upon landing at Ford were swiftly rebombed and refuelled ready to return to the fray. During the entire day there was no let-up in operations but it dismayed the aircrews to see the slaughter that was going on below.

As dusk fell, the last of the Bostons returned to Ford. Weary aircrews stretched their limbs and after debriefing, headed for bed. It had not been a particularly good day, with 174 Squadron, using Ford for the day, losing six Hurricanes and Nos. 88 and 418 Squadrons losing a Boston each with many more damaged. The news that same night did nothing to dispel the gloom felt by all. Dieppe had not only failed but there had also been a terrible loss of life. To crown it all, Ford was subjected to the first air raid in some time.

No. 141 Squadron had played no part in 'Jubilee' and had suffered various internal troubles since its arrival at Ford. Towards the end of 1942 it received a new Commanding Officer, Wing Commander J R D 'Bob' Braham. Being given the brief 'Get it back in shape and if there is anything you want, you will be given all the help you require', Bob Braham came south to Ford. For some reason a friendly sort of rivalry sprang up between 141 and the FIU. On occasions, some of the pilots of the former flew with the experimental unit and when on clear nights the German raiders came over, both units were airborne and hoping to outdo each other on their scores.

Shortly after the arrival of 141 Squadron at Ford, Braham and his AI operator, 'Sticks' Gregory were airborne in their Beaufighter one very clear night. The GCI station at Sandwich had picked up a contact crossing the coast and had vectored the Beaufighter to within visual distance of a Dornier 217. Switching on his radar in the cockpit, 'Sticks' Gregory kept trace of the Dornier as it took evasive action. Bringing his aircraft round to the best position, Braham opened fire at the same time as the rear gunner of the Dornier. Luckily the German's fire was none too accurate whereas the Beaufighter's shells struck home. As it began to dive, flames were seen rapidly spreading along the aircraft, and with a tremendous splash it fell into the sea. This type of combat was typical of any night throughout the year and together with the FIU, 141 completed a very good team.

605 Squadron had remained at Ford after 'Jubilee' but the detachment from 107 had departed shortly after to Great Massingham. There was very little change but a fair amount of activity over the Christmas period as 1943 arrived and the real path to victory began.

On 31st January, the defeated German 6th Army surrendered at Stalingrad, this important milestone having very little effect on Ford. No. 141 Squadron, after a very successful stay moved on to Predannack on 18th February 1943 and were replaced by No. 604 (County of Middlesex) Squadron who flew to Ford the same afternoon. With a noted decrease in enemy night raids, some of the squadron Beaufighters were diverted to intruder operations over the enemy airfields in Northern France. One month later it was all change at the airfield when 605 went to Castle Camps to convert to Mosquitos and in their place came No. 418 (City of Edmonton) Squadron of the Royal Canadian Air Force. They had already converted to the Mosquito II, and flying previously from Bradwell Bay they had found some success. Flying from Ford they were to find even greater success.

For No. 604 it was a short stay as they took their Beaufighters to Scorton on the 24th April 1943. Once again, that same afternoon it was the turn of No. 256 Squadron to bring their Beaufighter VIFs down from Woodvale, but their days with this faithful type were numbered as they began conversion to the Mosquito XII in May. This mark of Mosquito was really a Mk II with a very updated airborne radar known as a centimetric radar with the classification of AI Mk VIII. Of the aircraft first flying in March 1943, 256 were among the first night-fighter squadrons to get the aircraft. It was to prove its worth four nights later after the arrival of 256 at Ford when one of them destroyed a Dornier 217 over Worthing.

The FIU, quietly carrying on with their test and experimental work had gained the title of the 'Operational Flying Club'. Although a test unit, they regularly carried out operational patrols at night with a great deal of success. It was however, a more relaxed unit than the regular squadrons and a posting to it was rather looked upon as a special favour. The officers' mess at Ford was a requisitioned girls' school known as Tortington Hall. Both the FIU and the other squadrons on the airfield used the mess for eating and sleeping. It was the latter that sparked off a huge response when it was found that above each bed was a notice 'If anyone needs a mistress in the night, ring three times'. In anticipation of the military response the bells were taken out of use before even the first RAF personnel arrived!

August saw a lack of action at Ford and defensive patrols brought little contact with the enemy. For the FIU it was a very quiet time as regards kills and the unit applied for offensive status. This was refused on the grounds that as their aircraft carried top secret experimental apparatus, the risk of being shot down over enemy territory and the equipment falling into the hands of the Germans was far too great. Thus they had to be content with carrying on with their defensive work. It was not however entirely dull for incorporated within the FIU was a Navy night-fighting development unit which flew a selection of Naval aircraft including Fulmars and Rocs. It was not unusual to see the RAF pilots fly the Naval aircraft and vice-versa but of far greater attraction was the fact that the Navy had Wrens attached to it. This fact alone made sure there was inter-service union!

By August, 256 Squadron were ready to move on. They left Ford on the 25th for Woodvale and then to Luqa in Malta. They had enjoyed a very successful period at the airfield but the excitement of going overseas made leaving less of a wrench. By September 1943 the war was going very well, with Allied landings in the toe of Italy and then at Salerno a month later. At the same time, Italy declared war on Germany and although still a long way off, victory was definitely in sight.

29 Squadron had converted to the Mosquito V1 in July 1943 whilst at Bradwell Bay. They had achieved a great deal of success and notoriety during 1941/2 whilst flying from West Malling in Kent in Beaufighters. The V1 mark of Mosquito that they now flew was a day and night intruder aircraft and could also be used in the fighter/ bomber rôle. By October they were flying the Mk. XIII and due to the new mark of AI, were not allowed to undertake offensive operations over France. The CO, Wing Commander R E X Mack, DFC, protested strongly and towards the end of the year, 29 were allowed to penetrate over Northern France and the Low Countries attacking both enemy aircraft and airfields.

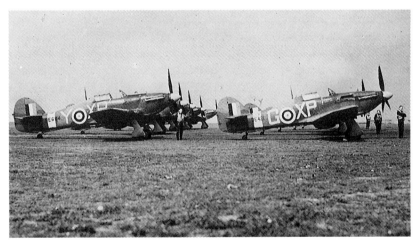

In March 1942, a detachment of Hurricane IIBs of 174 Squadron arrived at Ford from Manston. They were employed on fighter/bomber missions against enemy shipping and coastal targets. This continued until December 1943 when the squadron was withdrawn for Army Co-operation training in preparation for re-equipping with Typhoons (Imperial War Museum).

77

The 15th November 1943 will forever be remembered as the day someone destroyed Fighter Command. Not quite literally but for some reason, Fighter Command was renamed the Air Defence of Great Britain, a name that had been used during the 1930s. All of this had something to do with the reorganisation of the chain of command in preparation for a planned invasion of Europe sometime during 1944. The idea of throwing away such an established command did not go down well in the service and sometime later the name hurriedly reverted to Fighter Command. At Ford, the idea of losing the title appalled everybody.

As 1944 approached and with the war going in the Allies favour, the talk was indeed of an invasion on the European mainland. As a prelude to this and acting on a comment made by the Commander-in-Chief of Bomber Command, Air Marshall 'Bomber' Harris that he could wreck Berlin from end to end, a major bombing offensive began on the German capital. With the first raid taking place on 18th November 1943, the offensive continued until 26th March 1944. It cost Bomber Command more than 500 aircraft and many lives lost but did eventually bring the end of the war closer. In retaliation however, the Luftwaffe, acting on direct orders from Hitler, carried out a major assault on London and the south east of England. Known as 'Operation Steinbock' it began in January 1944. For 29 Squadron and the FIU at Ford it meant better business than they had seen for at least six months. The night of 21st/22nd January 1944 was particularly busy with over 400 enemy aircraft making raids on the capital. 29 Squadron were scrambled first from Ford and during the next few hours accounted for no less than nine kills. The FIU were also taking part and for the airfield it was to prove a very good and busy night.

This pattern of attacks continued throughout the rest of January and into February, the 24th proving a good bag when another five enemy aircraft were shot down. But it was also the night that Wing Commander Mack, the CO of 29, was shot down. The German assault was to last until April but after an excellent stay at Ford, 29 were posted to Drem in Scotland on 29th February. A few hours after they left having beaten up the airfield as was customary for a successful squadron stay, No. 456 Squadron brought their Mosquito XVIIIs in from Fairwood Common. Ford was entering a period of intense activity as the drive towards victory continued.

As early as April 1943, a headquarters for the planned invasion of

78

Europe had been set up. It consisted of Americans and British who were only too well aware of the disaster back in 1942 and a failure of this planned assault could well set the war back many years. It had to be got right.

As Ford once again became enveloped in a cloak of security, after three long years the FIU prepared to move to Wittering in order to continue their invaluable work. 'Operation Overlord' as the invasion was now labelled, had no place for experimental units and it was with heavy hearts that they left Ford in April.

The airfield now became classified as No. 122 Airfield and came under the umbrella of the Allied Expeditionary Air Force. By 15th April, the first of the squadrons incorporated within 122 Airfield had arrived in the shape of Nos. 19, 65 (East India) and 122 (Bombay). All three were equipped with the Rolls Royce engined North American Mustang III of which No. 19 had been the first to receive the type. 122 Airfield had previously been stationed at Gravesend where the aircraft had been fitted with a Spitfire type sliding hood in place of the usual upwards hinging canopy. As soon as the settling in was accomplished, 122 Airfield began 'Ranger' operations over France. These deep penetration flights enabled the Mustangs to engage any target they saw and 122 Squadron roamed as far as the Swiss border managing to shoot down seven enemy aircraft and damaging another with no loss to themselves.

By April, the Mustangs were carrying out fighter/bomber attacks on France with Nos. 65 and 122 Squadrons dropping 500 lb bombs on marshalling yards and enemy gun sites. It was all change a month later when No. 19 moved to Southend and 65 and 122 Squadrons to Funtington. The arrival of the Spitfire IXBs of No. 125 Airfield caused quite a stir as they roared in over the southern boundary. Comprising Nos. 132 (City of Bombay), 453 and 602 (City of Glasgow) Squadrons, the Spitfires carried out many offensive sorties over France, Belgium and Holland in conjunction with attacks on the 'Noball' sites where it was known the V1 launch ramps were.

Prior to the D Day landings, Ford became very crowded as 125 Airfield was joined by No. 144 Wing of the RCAF. Nos. 441 (Silver Fox), 442 (Caribou) and 443 (Hornet) Squadrons flew in from the ALG at Funtington with Spitfire IXBs. Arriving on 13th May, they were soon carrying out 'Roadsteds, Rodeos and Ramrods' attacking railways, highways, V1 launch sites and German radar sites. For the enemy, there was no respite from aerial bombardment.

D Day was originally scheduled for 5th June 1944, but had to be postponed for 24 hours because of unfavourable weather conditions which abated only slightly on the 6th, but it was a case of go then or postpone 'Overlord' for at least two weeks.

On the eve of the 6th, the Supreme Commander of the AEF, General Dwight Eisenhower stated: 'I am quite positive we must give the order . . . I don't like it but there it is . . . I don't see how we can possibly do anything else.' Nothing else could be done and the order was given. At dawn on 6th June 1944 D Day began with the Allies landing on the heavily fortified coast of France.

All the squadrons at a grossly overcrowded Ford took part. Some provided top cover for the landing craft, some over the landing zones themselves and others flew inland to prevent German bombers and fighters attacking the landing troops. On the first day of the invasion, the Allied Air Forces had around 3,000 bombers and 5,000 fighters and fighter/bombers at their disposal. The main Luftwaffe unit, Luftflotte III had barely 810 aircraft. Although reinforcements arrived around 10th June, it was too late to prevent the aim of 'Overlord' being achieved. By night it was the turn of the Mosquitos of No. 456 Squadron to continue the attack against a very confused enemy. They achieved enormous success when they shot down four Heinkel 177s on 7th June, repeating the success the next night when they shot down three more for no loss. To the enemy it was becoming quite obvious that an Allied victory could not be far away.

With the excitement over, Ford returned to its normal sedate atmosphere as 144 Wing departed to B3/Ste-Croix-sur-Mer on 15th June with 125 Airfield going to B11/Longues on the 25th. It had been a very hectic period but one that had achieved enormous advances for the Allies.

On Monday 12th June 1944, a weapon of undescribable terror was unleashed upon the British public. In the early hours of the morning, the first V1 (Doodlebug) was launched against the British mainland. 456 Squadron were already at Ford to combat this new menace and they were joined on 20th June by 96 Squadron who brought their Mosquito XIIIs over from West Malling in Kent. It was a dangerous job to shoot the robots out of the sky for the explosion invariably damaged the attacking aircraft. Some time later a new method of destruction was devised when the attacking aircraft formated

80

A German JU88 bomber (MAP).

alongside the V1, bringing his wing to just under the short stubby wing on the rocket. The air flow over the wings then tipped the V1 downward and it plunged to earth. However, 96 became very good at using the conventional method and their score at the end of the month had reached 49.

With the departure of the D Day squadrons, Ford was home to 456 and 96 until the arrival of 129 (Mysore) Squadron on 24th June and two Polish squadrons 306 (Turun) and 315 (Deblin) a day later. Once again the noise of the Mustang III returned to the airfield as they immediately began offensive patrols over enemy lines. They stayed just a little time for as the daily launchings of V1s were increasing all the time, they moved to Brenzett ALG in Kent and carried out anti-diver operations. It was the Poles who flew into Ford once again on 16th July when No. 131 (Polish) Wing arrived from the Sussex ALGs. Nos. 302 (Poznan), 308 (Krakow) and 317 (Wilno) were ready to join in the push towards victory. No. 302 Squadron had the distinction of being one of the only two Polish squadrons to have fought in the Battle of Britain, the other being No. 303 (Kosciusk). The Poles had proved themselves to be strong and resilient in battle and despite their initial lack of understanding English, intensive instruction in the language proved worthwhile. They carried out a few offensive sorties from Ford before flying to the landing strips in France on 4th August.

In their place came No. 132 Wing comprising Nos. 66, 127, 331 (Norwegian) and 322 (Norwegian). Flying Spitfire IXs, they too departed to B.16 Villon les Buissons on 20th August as the Allied advance towards Germany continued. The airfield was left once again to 96 and 456 squadrons but with the V1 attacks petering out as the Allies overran the launch sites, 96 departed to Odiham on 24th September 1944. 456 were not on their own for long as the FIU returned once more to Ford. They arrived with a detachment of 746 FAA Squadron and immediately the two units combined to form the Night Fighter Development Wing. Sadly the name FIU was left to history but the rôle of the new units remained the same. They flew Mosquitos, Beaufighters and several naval aircraft, and as if it were an indication of the future rôle of Ford, naval uniforms seemed to be in great abundance.

Though the V1 launchings from France were assumed to have ended on 1st September 1944, a few were still being launched from sites in Holland. Far more troublesome however were the airborne V1 launches which Hitler authorised as a last minute desperate attempt to bring London to its knees. They were launched from Heinkel 111s and to counteract this new threat, 456 reverted back to anti-diver operations. Once again they achieved a lot of success during October and November but at the end of the year when the airborne landings ceased, 456 took their Mosquitos to Church Fenton in Yorkshire. Their time at Ford had been very successful.

Christmas that year was celebrated with an air of expected victory. The Allies were pushing further and further towards Berlin and with the Yalta Conference between Roosevelt, Stalin and Churchill taking place between 4th and 11th February 1945 agreeing to future world policies in the lead-up to and after victory, life tasted just a little sweeter.

The Development Wing continued a lone existence at Ford as strategically the airfield was of no further use. On 30th April in a prelude to the end of the war, Hitler took his own life. The final Allied offensive, launched earlier in the month, could not be stopped and the German military sued for an armistice. Victory in Europe came on 8th May 1945 and the entire country celebrated. Although war was to continue in the Pacific for another four months, the dropping of two atomic bombs, one on Hiroshima and the other on Nagasaki, brought this to a swift conclusion, and on 2nd September 1945 World War Two ended.

With the end of hostilities, the Development Wing had transferred to Tangmere by the end by July and Ford ceased to be a No. 11 Group Fighter Command station on the 31st. Being of no further use as a fighter airfield, it was transferred back to the Admiralty and the name HMS Peregrine was resurrected. Its principal function was to act as a shore-based training establishment for squadrons temporarily disembarked from carriers. This, together with a Naval Service Trials Unit, ensured that the airfield was once again in the front line. Ford continued to be operational until 1958, when the Navy decided to concentrate the airfield's activities at other, better equipped, bases.

Today Ford is an open prison. It is more readily recognisable as an airfield from the air but parts of the perimeter track and the runway have survived for us to see. Many of the Naval buildings still exist, now in use by the Home Office. Housing is steadily encroaching onto the airfield but to the historian and many others, Ford will always be remembered as HMS Peregrine, one of the nicest shore-bases of the Navy.

4

THORNEY ISLAND

Although Thorney Island is on the fringe of the county and sometimes indicated as being in Hampshire, for the purposes of this book
I have chosen to include it in Sussex. Thorney Island must surely
hold a place in the writer's heart for it was here as a fledgeling Air
Cadet in 1954, that I took my first flight whilst at annual camp. The
airfield ceased flying during 1975 but did not sink into total obscurity
for it became a home for units of the Royal Artillery. During its
existence it was a very busy airfield and a memorial plaque situated
close to the Officers' Mess commemorates its beginning.

Shortly after its completion in 1938 (see Chapter One), Thorney
transferred from Coastal Command to No. 17 (Training) Group and
the School of General Reconnaissance formed to train GR pilots. The
Munich crisis of September 1938 brought the airfield to a war footing
as No. 42 Squadron left for Thornaby and the silver Ansons of the
training squadron were hastily camouflaged, armed with bombs and
dispersed around the perimeter of the airfield.

With the return of Prime Minister Neville Chamberlain from
Munich the situation was relaxed. Life returned to normal as No. 42
returned but the transfer back to Coastal Command on 1st November
1938 made everyone realise that the peace gained by Chamberlain
was only temporary.

Training was resumed but even this had an air of urgency as the
radio broadcasts relayed the tense atmosphere of every country in
Europe as the German war machine gathered momentum. No. 42
moved to a new base at Bircham Newton on 12th August 1939 and
was immediately replaced by the Ansons of No. 48 Squadron who

arrived from Eastchurch. Whilst the main bulk of the squadron remained at Thorney, detachments were sent to Detling, Guernsey and Carew Cheriton. Coastal Command was beginning its war.

On that fateful Sunday, Thorney Island joined the rest of the world and listened to Neville Chamberlain's broadcast. At least now everyone knew and as if to accentuate this fact, both 22 and 28 Squadrons began immediate anti U-boat patrols over the Channel. Doubtless the period known as the 'Phoney War' allowed all the training to be put into practice as the RAF prepared for war.

It had long been known that the Ansons and Vildebeestes flown by the two squadrons at Thorney were basically obsolete and when confronted by a vastly superior enemy war machine would last no time at all. The aircraft planned to take Coastal Command into the war first flew on 15th April 1938, and one year later No. 22 Squadron at Thorney Island received the first of the new Bristol Beaufort torpedo bombers. Constructed with an all-metal stressed skin, it carried a crew of four with a maximum speed of 265 mph at 6,000 ft and was armed with two 0.303 guns in a nose and dorsal turret as well as being able to carry bombs or torpedoes. It was a very potent, much needed aircraft for the command. 22 Squadron converted to the type during early 1940 but made very few operational sorties from Thorney. They moved to North Coates on 8th April and carried out Coastal Command's first mine-laying sortie on the 15th. No. 42

Dunkirk 1940 – a defeat renowned for the gallantry of its evacuation of stranded troops. No. 48 Squadron flying Ansons gave protection to the rescuing ships and aircraft (Kent Messenger).

Squadron returned to the base on 28th April bringing their Beauforts in from Bircham Newton at the same time as the airfield was greatly expanded, eventually occupying the entire island!

As the Battle of Britain began, the evacuation of the BEF from Dunkirk was high on the list for 48 Squadron. They flew their Ansons over the beaches giving some comfort to the army below that at least the RAF was there. In June they converted to the Beaufort but due to problems with the Taurus engines, they were not flown operationally.

48 were joined on 10th June by a detachment of 235 Squadron who brought the first Blenheim 1Fs to Thorney. Flying in from Detling, they were joined by the Blenheims of 236 Squadron who came in from Middle Wallop three weeks later. Both units carried out fighter and reconnaisance duties with some success in shooting down the enemy but it was the Blenheim IVs of 59 Squadron that caused the most damage. Arriving at Thorney on 3rd July, they immediately came under the umbrella of Army Co-operation and commenced bombing attacks against French ports. Similar operations were carried out by the detachments of 59 Squadron operating from Manston, Bircham Newton and Detling.

Tuesday 13th August, 'Eagle Day', dawned mainly fair with early morning mist and drizzle. Over the Channel, light cloud had developed, this in turn holding up the initial onslaught although several units were on their way to their targets. Of little use to the Luftwaffe was the fact that the German intelligence service had classed all Fleet Air Arm, Training Command and Coastal Command airfields as fighter bases. Thus much of the attack power would be wasted on non-fighter sites. Thorney Island was not included in the initial attacks although a stray JU 88, possibly from KG 54 which had attacked airfields in Hampshire, did drop a cluster of bombs on the airfield. They did little damage but on the 16th, another JU 88 strayed over after attacking Gosport and dropped a bomb, managing to hit a hangar containing aircraft which were burnt out. All of this was a prelude to Sunday 18th August when Thorney received a very large raid.

German formations had been over the UK since early morning mainly bombing Kent airfields. In the early afternoon it was the turn of Luftflotte 3 under the command of Generalfeldmarschall Hugo Sperrle to attack airfields in the Hampshire and West Sussex area.

Gosport suffered badly once again but it was the 1st and 2nd Gruppes of Stg 1 and 2 escorted by ME 109s that subjected Thorney to a devastating attack.

The week long effort by the Luftwaffe to destroy Fighter Command in line with the promise made by Goering to Hitler ended in a flourish on this significant Sunday. Although the raids were going on all morning over the south east, it was at 2 pm that a large force was plotted approaching the Isle of Wight. Operating from Caen, the Stukas of Stg 77 escorted by the 109s of JG 27 from Plumetot held a steady course as they made for Poling radar station, Ford and Thorney Island. Crossing the coast, the force split with Hauptmann Meisel taking his Gruppe to attack Thorney. Part of the fighter escort also broke and joined the 28 Stukas as they came closer and closer to their intended target. Within minutes the runways at Thorney Island were plainly visible as the aircraft went into their classic line astern formation. As they did so, 43 Squadron arrived on the scene and immediately went into the attack. Below them 235 Squadron, based at the airfield, scrambled some of their Blenheim fighters in great haste as the armada approached but it was a futile effort for it was far too late for them to do anything as the Stukas began their dive. By now the sky was full of fighters and bombers weaving in amongst each other as the air was filled with the sound of gunfire. Although the tightly held formation of the enemy had been broken up as each aircraft fought for its own survival, the attack was still carried out with deadly precision and devastating results.

Many people in the surrounding area were finishing Sunday lunch when Thorney Island was hit. Even the drone of the enemy overhead could not distract many from the main family meal of the week. Only when the 'crump-crump' of exploding bombs was heard coming nearer did they retire with their pudding to a safer part of the house. For some it was none too soon as with their characteristic scream, the Stukas levelled out and released their bombs. Two hangars received direct hits reducing them to rubble in seconds, including the three Ansons inside them. One salvo hit a fuel dump and in one terrific explosion the fuel ignited, throwing billowing clouds of black smoke and flames high into the sky. Despite the artificial smokescreen, the second wave of Stukas dived and dropped their bombs, one of them landing very near to a shelter and injuring five civilian workmen who were working on the airfield expansion. Overhead could be heard the sharp staccato of machine guns as the RAF threw their fighters into the enemy force and then as quickly as the raid had begun, the sky was empty as the Luftwaffe turned and headed for home. On the ground the sounds of crackling fire and secondary explosions together with a lot of shouting filled the air.

The Luftwaffe suffered badly as 43, 152, 601 and 602 Squadrons arrived to do battle. This they did with the Germans losing ten Stukas and several 109s. This day heralded the end of Stuka operations over Britain and it was also significant because the 2nd Gruppe of JG 57 lost one of its aces, Hauptmann Horst Tietzen. JG 26 also lost Lt. Gerhard Muller-Duhe and JG 3 lost Oberleutnant Helmut Tiedmann.

With the raid over, work began on filling in the craters. Although badly pitted, the airfield remained operational and raids by the Thorney Island squadrons were able to take place the same night.

The next large attack came on 23rd August when three JU 88s flew over late one evening and dropped their bombs, none causing death but with a fair amount of damage. 602 Squadron had been scrambled from Westhampnett to deal with the raiders but whilst flying in an area of low cloud, Spitfire X4160 flown by P/O T G F Ritchie collided with an unknown aircraft but was able to make it back to base. The next day brought a tragic case of mistaken identity when three Blenheims of 235 Squadron were attacked on a routine patrol by Hurricanes of No. 1 (RCAF) Squadron. Blenheim Z5736 crashed on landing back at Thorney, the crew of Sgt. K Naish and Sgt. W G Owen surviving. Blenheim N3531 landed safely back at base but Blenheim T1804 crashed into Bracklesham Bay with P/O D N Woodger lost and Sgt. D L Wright killed. Though incidents like this were rare, they did happen throughout the war mainly due to poor aircraft recognition. The tragedy shook the airmen and women at Thorney far more than the German raids and it took some time for the station to shake off the loss and get back to normal.

September 1940 saw some relief from the bombing by the enemy and it also saw the detachment of 42 Squadron with Beauforts still in residence with Nos. 59 and 235 still flying Blenheims. Something of a novelty occurred at Thorney on 11th September when 812 Squadron of the Fleet Air Arm brought their Fairey Swordfish to operate from the airfield for mine-laying operations in coastal areas of Belgium, Holland and France. Led by Lt./Cdr W E Waters, DFC, RN, they were temporarily attached to Coastal Command for this period

A superb formation shot of 235 Squadron flying the Blenheim Mk. IVF, several of which were used at Thorney (Imperial War Museum).

which proved very successful for the squadron, despite the Navy pilots not liking their aircraft being serviced by airmen!

More Blenheim IVs came to Thorney Island on 24th November when 53 Squadron arrived from Detling. With detachments sent to Bircham Newton and St Eval, they joined with 59 Squadron in bombing enemy held ports. This pattern of attacks continued until 1941, the Christmas period being relatively calm as bad weather prevented both the Luftwaffe and the RAF from carrying out operations. Though not the subject of any further heavy raids by the Germans, Thorney Island was still a target for the odd JU 88 that could sneak in under cloud cover. These attacks continued into the New Year causing nothing but a nuisance as 812 Squadron, who had flitted between Thorney and North Coates for the past months, came back to the airfield on 12th January 1941. The next three months saw 53,

59 and the detachment of 235 Squadrons still in residence but on 20th March 1941 the partnership was split up when 53 moved down to St Eval. A month later a RCAF squadron, No. 404 (Buffalo) formed at Thorney with the Blenheim 1FV. They began training and were later joined by 407 (Demon) Squadron also of the RCAF, equipped with Blenheim 1s. Although they converted to the Lockheed Hudson whilst at Thorney, neither they nor 404 carried out any operations. They were posted to the ends of the country with 404 going to Castletown on 20th June and 407 going to North Coates on 8th July. In their place No. 415 (Swordfish) Squadron of the RCAF formed at Thorney on 20th August 1941 with Beauforts. It was a time of rapid changes for the airfield.

No. 22 Squadron came winging back on 25th June bringing their Beauforts in just after dawn. They were now engaged in the torpedo strike role, and with the earlier problems with their engines sorted out were to enjoy a successful period. They began operations immediately, attacking enemy shipping that was hugging the Belgian and French coastline. Another Beaufort squadron arrived in the form of 217 Squadron who flew their aircraft up from St Eval on 29th October

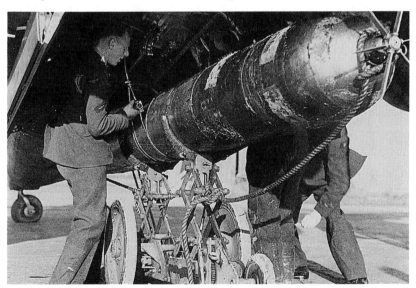

As the German fleet approached the English Channel, Beauforts of 217 Squadron were briefed to attack them with torpedoes (Crown).

90

1941. Three weeks later they converted to the Beaufort II which had the more reliable American Twin Wasp engines. Their motto was 'Woe to the unwary' and the success that they enjoyed in the torpedo strike rôle whilst operating from Thorney certainly proved that the enemy were sometimes very unwary.

With the end of 1941 fast approaching it was still a time of rapid squadron changes. 22 had departed to St Eval in October, 53 had also gone but 59, now flying the Hudson III and V were still resident. No. 235 had moved to Dyce whilst the Canadian 415 Squadron were still carrying out torpedo strikes from Thorney. Christmas 1941 saw the base still as a grass airfield but with Coastal Command getting heavier and more powerful aircraft, it became obvious that a concrete runway was desperately needed. Though there had been mention of further extensions to and an upgrading of Thorney, it was not to happen until well into the New Year.

Meantime, further changes had taken place as No. 280 Squadron formed at Thorney Island with the obsolete Anson to further the amount of ASR work being undertaken. 217 Squadron had sent

A practice torpedo drop off the Sussex coastline by a Beaufort of 42 Squadron (South Eastern Newspapers).

91

detachments of their Beauforts to St Eval, Manston, North Coates and Skitten. With the Christmas period over, the proposed update of Thorney became reality as the construction gangs moved in to commence work. This was to consist of a concrete runway together with perimeter track around the entire site. Work progressed well and by July a concrete runway of 6,090 ft running SW/NE had been finished and subsidiary runways running N/S and SE/NW were about to be started. The two damaged 'C' Type hangars were replaced by 17 large blisters and several extra workshops were built. It was a great improvement on the original site but all of this work took second place to one of the most hectic periods in the history of Thorney Island.

At 11 am on Monday 16th February 1942, a board of inquiry sat in private in the Whitehall Room, part of the Admiralty in London. The Government had been forced to conduct this inquiry under direct orders of Winston Churchill to find out what had gone wrong and why a particular operation had become known as the 'War's greatest blunder'. The date in question was 12th February 1942, the day the most powerful enemy battle fleet afloat sailed unscathed through the Straits of Dover, openly flouting the Royal Navy's supremacy in the Channel.

For some time an operation known as 'Channel Stop' had been in force and was intended to stop German shipping from passing through the English Channel. It had not been too successful but the Admiralty and the Air Ministry thought it essential that this operation should continue. For some time the German battle cruisers Scharnhorst, Prinz Eugen and Gneisenau had not been seen and the Royal Navy had wondered just where they were. Unbeknown to them, the fleet was hidden in Brest Harbour and was preparing for a dramatic breakout to travel through the Dover Straits and back to a port in Germany. If the plan succeeded, it would be the first time in 300 years that enemy ships had sailed within 18 miles of the English south coast. Information had already reached London that there was reason to expect that the battle cruisers would attempt to reach Germany by sailing through the Channel, but with the 'Channel Stop' operations London considered this highly improbable. However, just in case, Coastal Command were ordered to establish dusk-to-dawn reconnaissance flights over and off Brest. The operation was code-named 'Fuller' and in a signal from headquarters Coastal Command to all airfields within the command, Air Chief Marshal Sir Phillip Joubert said: 'Prior warning of a passage through the Channel may not be received. The intention is to destroy the major enemy units on passage from Brest to a German port. If practicable, the torpedo attack from Thorney Island will be launched to synchronise with the bombing attack in order to take advantage of the fighter cover provided for the bombers.'

As history records, the Germans did break out and there followed a tragic series of circumstances resulting in the death and posthumous award of the VC to Lt/Cdr. Eugene Esmond, the leader of an ill-fated Swordfish Squadron. Many of the same unit were also killed and in the annals of aviation tragedy it must rate as one of the worst incidents of the entire war.

Thorney Island had been put on full readiness the moment the signal relating to the possible breakout had been received. The radar stations high up on the cliffs at Beachy Head and Fairlight responded likewise and did in fact spot the gathering of the German escort vessels on their screens, but due to a series of unusual circumstances could not raise Dover by telephone to report the fact. Precious time had already been lost. By this time it was 10.20 am and with the raiders having left Brest at around 8.15 am, two hours had gone by with no formal identification being made and without the British military knowing of the battle cruisers whereabouts. The first indications of an enemy convoy in the Channel came when two reconnaissance Spitfires landed at Hawkinge and reported 30 to 40 ships being escorted by five destroyers or E-boats. Both pilots, Group Captain Victor Beamish and Wing Commander Boyd, failed to recognise either of the capital ships, and consequently 'Operation Fuller' was not put into action. In fact it was not until 11.25 am that formal recognition was acknowledged and the attack was finally put into action. At 12.18 pm the armed forces engaged the enemy for the first time when the Dover gun batteries opened up. They were followed by an attack by five Dover based MTBs but this, together with several other attempts later on, all came to nothing. The huge armada sailed on.

One of the more gallant attempts to slow or stop the German fleet was made by No. 825 Squadron of the FAA with their flimsy Swordfish aircraft. In their attack, most of the aircraft were shot down from the sky with the loss of their crews including their leader, Lt/Cdr.

93

The Swordfish, seemingly too fragile for aerial combat, took part in the abortive attempt to halt the progress of the German navy through the Channel. Many were lost with their crews. This flying example belongs to the Fleet Air Arm Historical Flight based at Yeovilton (Aviation Photo News).

Esmond who gained a posthumous VC for his gallantry. Both the Swordfish and the previous MTB attacks had passed over by 1 pm and it was felt that Coastal Command was now best situated for the next attempt to hit the enemy convoy. The seven Beauforts of 217 Squadron at Thorney Island were the closest to hand and plans for them to rendezvous with a fighter escort over Manston at 1.30 pm were put forward. Unfortunately, two of the aircraft were armed with bombs instead of torpedoes and a third aircraft was unserviceable. As considerable time would be lost changing the bombs it was eventually decided to send the four serviceable aircraft with the other three following later on. With problems arising at take-off, the Beauforts were late arriving at Manston and the fighters had gone to the target area ahead, being told to look out for the Beauforts when they arrived. Unfortunately the signal informing P/O Carson, the leader of the Thorney contingent, did not reach him due to the fact that it was sent by W/T (wireless telegraphy, ie: morse) to the Beauforts which had just recently had the newer R/T (radio telegraphy) radio installed. After circling Manston for some fifteen minutes, Carson led his aircraft out to sea in the general direction of his previous information. Unfortunately, two of his aircraft failed to see in which direction they should be flying and continued orbiting Manston awaiting further orders. Eventually running out of fuel, they landed at the airfield and upon being asked just what was going on, the crews amazed the Manston staff by saying they really did not know just what the operation was. 'Do you mean no-one has told you?' gasped the controller. 'No sir,' said the crews. No further time was wasted and the pilots were briefed as their aircraft were refuelled. They took off, an hour and a half late to join the other aircraft but with the clouds gathering the enemy would now be hard to find.

When they did eventually come across a force of FW 190s and ME 109s, they knew that they were near the German fleet but the hail of tracer fire from the fighters indicated that to put their torpedoes in exactly the right place would be no picnic. In the event, although the aircraft did finally release their missiles, no hits were registered and another torpedo attack had failed. Unscathed, the battle fleet sailed on.

In the meantime, the three aircraft left behind at Thorney Island arrived over Manston to meet the fighter escorts. Again, none of the pilots knew their target or even just where they were supposed to be going. One of them found it necessary to land, whereupon he was informed of the operation and when once again airborne, told the rest of the crews. They headed out to sea and shortly after came upon the fleet. Immediately they were enveloped in flak and were forced to fly over the Dutch coast to begin their run-in. The first Beaufort suffered badly from flak damage as it came in to drop its torpedo. Two of the crew were injured and the torpedo release gear was hit, causing the pilot to abort his attempt and head back to Manston. He managed to cross the Channel, but the coastal gunners at Ramsgate mistook the aircraft for a Heinkel and further damage was done to the Beaufort. With great skill however, the pilot landed his aircraft safely.

The second Beaufort suffered very similar mishaps when it too was hit by enemy fighters and could not release its torpedo. Deciding to return to Manston, the aircraft arrived in the overhead when the pilot realised he could not lower his undercarriage. Circling the airfield he tried desperately to release it for he knew that to attempt a belly landing with a live torpedo aboard would be suicidal. It proved useless and a soft landing was the only answer. Coming in low and slow, the crew prepared for the worst. As the Beaufort hit the grass, the torpedo was wrenched from its cradle and fell clear of the aircraft. It did not explode and a weary and sweating crew emerged from the crashed aircraft.

The third Beaufort, piloted by Sgt. Rowt who was making his first operational flight, dropped its torpedo successfully but was badly shot up by FW 190s as it emerged from the enemy smoke-screen. Struggling to remain airborne, the pilot made a safe landing at Manston. For 217 Squadron, it had been a gallant attempt which had not hindered the enemy in any way. Although further Beauforts were deployed to Thorney Island from St Eval, they had no chance of attacking the enemy for by late afternoon the weather closed in.

The Germans however did not have total good luck for unknown to the British at the time, Scharnhorst had struck a mine and was temporarily out of action whilst her engineers repaired the damage. Minutes later, Gneisenau also struck a mine but it was too late in the day to carry out any further air attacks and for the Germans the 'Channel Dash', as it became known, was a success. For the British, it was a humiliating time and resulted in the aforementioned inquiry.

After the hectic period, 217 were posted to Leuchars on 6th March 1942 and a day later were on their way to the Far East. The Canadian 415 Squadron had exchanged their Beauforts for the Handley Page Hampden during January and were busy working up on the type. The big extensions at Thorney had been completed by March and were fully in use, the Hampdens happily using the new concrete runway.

A RNZAF squadron, No. 489, brought their Blenheims to Thorney on 8th March but immediately converted to the Hampden. Since its time as a night-bomber, this aircraft had been given a new lease of life and continued on operations with Coastal Command as a torpedo bomber. It gave a good account of itself against enemy shipping and proved to be a very versatile aircraft.

A complete contrast of aircraft moved to Thorney on 30th July when Spitfire VBs of No. 129 (Mysore) Squadron flew in from nearby West-hampnett. They had been undertaking offensive sweeps over the Channel but had flown to Thorney Island in preparation for

'Operation Jubilee', the ill-fated Dieppe landing. They were joined by No. 130 (Punjab) Squadron on 16th August bringing the airfield to a fighter status. The two squadrons carried Indian titles due to the fact that much of the equipment had been purchased with money subscribed by India and this was further strengthened when a proportion of its personnel came from the Indian Commonwealth.

As 19th June 1942 approached, the date set for the invasion of Dieppe, the airfield became cloaked in security. Briefings were carried out at the last possible moment on the 18th and at dawn the next day, the Spitfires of 129 were airborne on the first attack on enemy positions. During the sortie, a Spitfire of the squadron achieved the dubious distinction of being the first aircraft to be shot down during 'Jubilee' when the squadron met a force of FW 190s and gave a good account of themselves during the following dogfight.

No. 130 were over next to fly protection sorties over the armada of British ships below. When they returned it was 129 again who carried on the fight as they witnessed the carnage that was going on below. A fleet of 237 ships were off the French coast with more than 6,000 men, British and Canadian, struggling to get a foothold in Dieppe. The assault was to finally prove a failure from which only a third of the men were to return. Like the 'Channel Dash', it was to result in an inquiry to find out just what went wrong.

The Luftwaffe returned to bomb Thorney Island on the 18th August 1942 when several aircraft came in low under cloud cover. Whilst it caused a fair amount of damage, it was really the last sizeable raid on the airfield. With 'Jubilee' over, No. 130 Squadron returned to Perranporth on 20th August whilst 129 hung on until 25th September before returning to Grimsetter. The Spitfires had enjoyed a fairly successful stay, but any jubilation was overshadowed by what had happened at Dieppe.

With the completion of the long awaited concrete runway and hardstandings back in the New Year, Thorney Island was now able to accept just about any type of aircraft. This being the case, a very different type arrived at the airfield on 18th August in the shape of the Armstrong Whitley VII. This aircraft had been one of the major stays of Bomber Command during the early years of the war but like the Hampden, had been superseded by newer and better aircraft. Again like the Hampden, it saw a resurgence of use when Coastal Command used it in the anti-submarine role. The Whitley GR

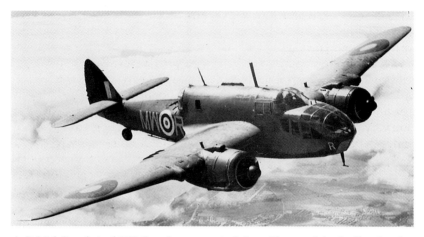

A Bristol Beaufort of 217 Squadron on patrol from Thorney Island. Shortly after arrival they converted to the Mk II but they continued to fly the type until August 1944. After early teething troubles with the engines, Beauforts were employed on attacks on enemy shipping and minelaying (MAP).

Mk. VII first entered service with the Command at the end of 1940 with 502 Squadron at Aldergrove and ·eventually four Coastal Command squadrons were to receive it.

No. 612 (County of Aberdeen) Squadron of the auxiliary air force brought their aircraft to Thorney from Reykjavik in Iceland and after a brief period to settle in began anti-submarine patrols over the Channel approaches. They were joined by previous occupants No. 59 who returned to Thorney with the Hudson III but quickly converted to the Consolidated Liberator III. These American aircraft had been destined for the French Air Force but with France out of the war, the order had been taken over by the RAF. It eventually proved to be one of the most effective aircraft used by Coastal Command against the enemy submarine. 59 were glad to be back at Thorney but with these large aircraft dispersed all around the airfield, the base appeared to be fast becoming a bomber park.

Another Liberator Squadron reformed at Thorney on 1st August 1942 when No. 86 were established to carry out the task of an Operational Training Unit on the aircraft. Many fresh aircrew personnel arrived and the airfield became very busy. With very little population that close to the airfield, the sounds of heavy engines only brought

98

forth a few complaints from civilians, even though with the war gradually going in the Allies favour the amount of flying had increased dramatically.

September 1942 saw No. 612 leave for Wick to carry on anti-submarine patrols off the Scottish coast and it also saw the return of Spitfires when No. 131 (County of Kent) Squadron flew their VBs in from nearby Tangmere, the fighters and bombers working side by side very well. The FAA returned once more on 7th September acting under the control of No. 16 Group. Nos. 816 and 819 Squadrons had re-equipped with Fairey Swordfish IIs and were briefed to carry out night operations in minelaying in the North Sea and later the English Channel. They stayed for about a month before returning to the fold of the FAA and back to carrier operations.

As the fourth Christmas of war approached, the thoughts of everyone turned to just what the future held. The war was now being pushed back to the continent and although the Dieppe operation had proved a failure, plans were already in hand for a new offensive. The season was celebrated with a new feeling of a future victory. The weather, very unseasonable, ensured that operations continued for both the RAF and the Luftwaffe so for Thorney the respite was very brief.

Before the Christmas period however, the Hampdens of 415 Squadron returned on 11th November 1942 to carry on their anti-shipping strikes. This time it was to be a stay of a year and two further conversions to new types. Just after Christmas, the FAA returned when 836 Squadron commanded by Lt. Cdr. R W Slater DSC RN arrived from St Merryn with Swordfish. They were briefed to continue the night operations in the English Channel so ably carried out by their predecessors.

With the New Year duly celebrated, 59 Squadron converted from the Liberator to the Boeing Fortress IIA and departed to Chivenor in Devon on 6th February 1943. They returned to Thorney on 27th March and carried on the anti-submarine patrols with the Fortress. On 31st January, the German 6th Army surrendered to the Russians at Stalingrad and the word was that the end of the war in North Africa could not be far off. Not that any of this had a great effect on Thorney Island but at least it indicated that the war was going the Allies way.

Back at their old haunt 59 Squadron were joined by the Liberator

Vs of No. 53. The former squadron sent a detachment to St Eval on 27th March and swiftly converted to the Liberator V in April. Both squadrons carried out many anti-submarine sweeps, sometimes in atrocious conditions and sometimes flying as far away as the Bay of Biscay. No U-boat was really safe from the prying eyes of 53 and 59!

With the return of the Canadian 415 Squadron in November 1942, the Hampden was fast becoming obsolete but it was not until September 1943 that they converted to the Wellington XIII. This was a specialised mark of Wellington for Coastal Command and although the type had basically completed its useful life in Bomber Command, it became an invaluable piece of equipment in the anti-submarine rôle. With the Mk. XIII, a return was made to ASV Mk. II radar and the masts began to appear on the top of the fuselage again.

The Swordfish of 836 Squadron had departed to Machrihanish on 16th March 1943 leaving Thorney once again to the RAF. The weather during the spring and summer was favourable to anti-submarine attacks and the station gradually began to make a name for itself in this type of operation. Many U-boats fell to the attacking aircraft of 53, 59 and 415 Squadrons. Although the FAA had left Thorney, surplus Fairey Albacores returned in October 1943 when A flight of 415 took them over for operations against German torpedo boats operating in the Channel and Dover Straits. The squadron moved on to Bircham Newton on the 15th November but the Albacores remained with a detachment left behind at Thorney. Further Wellingtons arrived on 25th October when No. 547 flew their XIs in from Davidstow Moor. They converted to the XIII sending a detachment to Aldergrove four days later before further converting to the Liberator V in November. The pace of war was suddenly quickening.

The New Year 1944 saw the Allies landing at Anzio, Italy and on 27th January, the Russians raised the siege of Leningrad. The progress to victory was gathering momentum and already there was talk of an Allied landing in Normandy. At Thorney Island it was a quiet time after the hectic period of changes during the past year. With 53, 59 and 547 Squadrons gone and just a detachment of 415 with Albacores remaining, the silence surrounding the airfield became unreal. It remained this way with just the occasional visitor to break the monotony for three months. Although the airfield was still retained by Coastal Command, the reason for the non-use became obvious when the Typhoons of 164 (Argentine/British) and

A familiar and awe-inspiring sight for the British public, especially during the Blitz. The trails denote the aftermath of a vicious aerial battle (South Eastern Newspapers).

193 (Fellowship of the Bellows – Brazil) moved to form No. 136 Airfield of No. 83 Group. Thorney had been taken over by the 2nd Tactical Air Force in preparation for the great assault. The two squadrons were further strengthened on 1st April when Nos. 183 (Gold Coast) and 609 (West Riding) arrived as No. 136 Airfield began offensive operations. The Typhoons, being new to the area, caused a considerable amount of consternation when, after a period of relative silence at Thorney, the surrounding area was drowned in the noise of many Sabre engines. April was a month of rapid squadron changes as the countdown to D Day began. The Typhoons were in action daily and by the end of the month, Nos. 123 and 136 Airfields were resident at Thorney. On 15th May they formed into wings and shortly after commenced operations against V1 and radar sites along the coast of France. Although the fighting was now very much on the offensive, several aircraft were lost when they were caught up in dogfights over heavily defended targets. 164 Squadron lost their leader, Squadron Leader A B Russell DFC in one of the sorties, the next day the squadron shot down two FW 190s.

In common with all the airfields, Thorney Island was cloaked in security as 6th June approached. Close by and all around the south coast, large numbers of landing craft could be seen as 'Operation Overlord' got under way. Originally scheduled for 5th June, the invasion was delayed by bad weather and preparations went ahead for the 6th. Just after midnight, the aircrews were briefed on their particular sorties, the two Thorney wings being given ground attack sweeps. At first light the air was filled with the noise of the Typhoons as the groundcrews ran them up ready for the pilots. No. 198 were first away and shortly after crossing the French coast attacked a German mobile column, claiming seven trucks destroyed. 183 were over in the next wave but suffered badly at the hands of the ME 109s and the German flak. No. 164 got caught in a dog-fight over Calais but succeeded in shooting down two FW 190s for no loss. Throughout 6th and 7th June, the Typhoons flew mission after mission as the Allied landings progressed. The next two weeks continued this hectic activity until 17th June when 164 moved to the ALG at Funtington followed the next day by Nos. 183, 198 and 609 Squadrons.

There was no respite as No. 140 Wing flew in to replace them. Composed of Nos. 21, 464 and 487 Squadrons, the wing flew the Mosquito FB VI and were part of No. 2 Group of the 2nd TAF. The VI mark had entered service originally with Fighter Command as a day and night intruder and it then went on to be the first Mosquito to enter service with Coastal Command. It was used in the anti-shipping rôle, and with rockets fitted beneath each wing it became a very potent, and for the enemy, lethal aircraft.

For the three squadrons that flew into Thorney on that summer day of 18th June 1944, fame had preceded their arrival for on 18th February, whilst operating from Hunsdon, 19 Mosquito VIs from Nos. 21, 464 and 487 Squadrons had carried out the memorable attack on the jail at Amiens led by Group Captain P C Pickard. The object of the raid was to make a breach in the prison walls, and as a result, 258 members of the French Resistance were able to make their escape. As the squadrons flew into Thorney Island, many of the station personnel made a point of being there to welcome them.

The wing began day and night intruder operations, sometimes flying as many as 15 to 20 sorties a day and ranging far over German held territory. Led by Group Captain P G Waykeman-Barnes DFC and Bar, the wing scored another success when on 14th July they

delivered nine tons of bombs very precisely on a Gestapo headquarters leaving the surrounding village of Bonnevil Matours totally
untouched. A similar operation of 1st August was equally successful
when a German barracks was destroyed in a pin-point attack. The
Mossies of 140 wing became very well known over enemy territory!
There were of course losses but the sheer scale of the attacks ensured
that the wing caused far more damage than they received.

The intruder hit and run operations continued throughout October
but with bad weather beginning to have an effect, the scale of
operations slowly ran down. The wing remained at Thorney over
Christmas, celebrating the season and the approaching victory with
a little more enthusiasm than in previous years. As 1945 dawned,
Warsaw was liberated and on the home front the German presence
over the British mainland became less and less. Despite the bad
weather that January 1945 brought, 21 Squadron shot down two of
what were to become the last few V1s launched against Britain. This
and a few intruder day raids were the last operations by the Wing
operating from Thorney Island. They had enjoyed a most productive
stay but with the availability of ALGs on the continent since D Day,
they left on 6th February 1945 for B87/Rosieres-en-Santerre.

Thorney was left to the Barracuda IIs of No. 810 Squadron and the
Mk. IIIs of 822 Squadron of the FAA. The aircraft had recently been
fitted with ASV M. XI and the move to Thorney was to try out the
new equipment on anti-shipping patrols in the English Channel.
They were joined by the Air Sea Warfare Development unit of the
FAA which was a newly formed squadron whose aims were to look
at and improve the methods of destruction of surface and underwater
vessels by air attack. The FAA remained the only occupants for some
time as the Grumman Avengers of No. 848 Squadron arrived from
Manston on 14th June led by Lt. Cdr. A V R Turney. They carried out
anti-shipping operations before going to Lee-on-Solent in August to
be replaced by Nos. 854 and 855 who continued the anti-shipping
sweeps; they in turn being replaced by several other FAA units
including Nos. 838, 842, 810 and 822 Squadrons.

Spitfires returned on 15th February 1945 when 278 Squadron flew
in from Martlesham Heath. Formed originally on 1st October 1941,
they carried out ASR duties, with the Spitfire later converting to the
Sea Otter II which they did whilst at Thorney. The very apt badge
depicting a lifebuoy with a seagull affrontee hovering and the motto

'From out of the sea to strike again' became very familiar and welcome sights to many aircrews who were forced to ditch in the cold English Channel. Detachments were sent to Hawkinge, Beccles and Exeter but with the end of the war in May, the squadron disbanded at Thorney on 14th October 1945.

The 9th April saw 703 Squadron reform as the Naval Flight of the RAF's Air-Sea Warfare Development Unit. It flew a variety of types initially, including Avengers, Barracudas, Fireflies, Hoverflies and Sea Mosquitos, known as Sea Hornets to the Navy. Commanded by Lt. Cdr. J H Dundas DFC, RN, they were to stay at Thorney for three years developing many new types of weapons to be used at sea. Four Mosquito FB VIs were detached to the station from 703 Squadron in June where they were temporarily joined with 703. The detachment was re-absorbed when the remainder of the squadron moved to Thorney on 4th September 1945.

And so the station ended the war as a FAA base although still under the cloak of Coastal Command. Germany formally surrendered on 7th May and with Mussolini being killed by partisans on 28th April and Hitler committing suicide on 30th April, the war in Europe came to an end. It was to continue for several more months in the Far East but to the forces stationed in the UK, it was all over.

Today the best way to see the airfield is from the air for with the Army in occupation, security allows no-one access to the island. The plaque commemorating the beginning of a very chequered career for Thorney Island remains but well inside the airfield boundary, it is seen by very few today. The records of Coastal Command can be justly proud of the many achievements of this island airfield and long may it remain an Army camp. For only this way can it hope to remain as a historical site.

5

WESTHAMPNETT

During the 1950s and early 60s Goodwood was known to all motor racing fans as the prima donna of the motor racing circuits. Previously an airfield known as Westhampnett, it was set in one of the loveliest surroundings in Sussex and played host to names like Reg Parnall, Mike Hawthorn and Stirling Moss. It closed when a number of near fatal accidents indicated that more stringent safety measures were needed. The cost proved to be prohibitive and the circuit closed in 1965, almost immediately to be reinstated as an airfield known by the name of Chichester/Goodwood.

The estate of Frederick Charles Gordon Lennox, the Duke of Richmond and Gordon, was situated just north of Chichester. When war became imminent, a large area of flat land was requisitioned by the Air Ministry as an emergency landing ground for nearby Tangmere. Not a lot happened until the Battle of Britain was about to start, when the ELG was upgraded to satellite status. The construction gangs moved in and four grass runways were laid with Sommerfeld Tracking, the dimensions being 1,500 yds SE-NW, 1,130 yds NE-SW, 1,030 yds N-S and a short 920 yds E-W. Several blister hangars were erected together with a watch office for airfield control. Not particularly popular with the airmen was the fact that whilst they were accommodated in canvas bell tents, the officer's mess was the manor house of Shopwyke Hall!

Although just a satellite and therefore not intended to be a front line airfield, Westhampnett was very well equipped and it was clearly earmarked for major use which began on 31st July 1940 when No. 145 Squadron moved their Hurricanes in from Tangmere. They had been

ME 109s prepare for take-off. They escorted the bombers which attacked British airfields such as Westhampnett with devastating results before turning their attention to the cities (MAP).

in the thick of the fighting during the opening phases and had tackled the Luftwaffe over the Channel convoys. Nothing was to change with the move, as immediately after settling in at Westhampnett they were scrambled to defend their old base.

Thursday 1st August dawned fair in most districts with a little cloud over the Straits of Dover. This dispersed during the day, and shortly before 1 pm a convoy made its way through the Channel. As it passed Hastings, two plots were picked up by the Fairlight radar station and the Tangmere controller scrambled two sections of Hurricanes from 145. They made contact off the coast with a JU 88 from the 2nd Gruppe of KG 76 operating from Creil and a Henschell 126. Immediately a fight began, resulting in the JU 88 receiving a lot of damage with one of the crew, Feldwebel Kohl, being injured and eventually dying. The aircraft managed to reach its own base but not so lucky was the Henschell 126 which was quickly dispatched to the bottom of the Channel. However, the rear gunner on the German aircraft managed to fire a shot at Hurricane P3155 and it, too, crashed into the Channel killing the pilot, Sub Lieutenant I H Kirstin, an exchange pilot from the Fleet Air Arm.

The next few days saw very sporadic action from the Luftwaffe and 145 were not scrambled by the controller. On the airfield itself, the construction gangs returned to carry out surface work for additional drainage. Previous downpours had tended to make Westhampnett very unsuitable for Hurricane operations and the squadron had frequent days back at Tangmere. With the Channel shipping still receiving the unwanted attention of the enemy, Friday 8th August proved a disastrous day for 145.

On the evening of the 7th, a convoy of 20 ships had left the Thames estuary intending to sail through the Channel Straits to Swanage. Codenamed 'CW 9 – Peewit', it was escorted by a number of naval vessels and was one of the more important convoys to attempt to sail through the Channel. Hugging the coastline, Peewit slowly made its way but the German radar, high on the cliffs of France, had noted its slow progress. Just before dawn on the 8th, a flotilla of German E-boats attacked, reducing the convoy by three ships and inflicting damage on two of the others. By first light, the Luftwaffe Luftflotte III had been alerted and a signal was sent to Generalmajor Wolfram Freiherr von Richthofen, the commander of Fliegerkorps VIII at his headquarters at Deauville. At all costs he must sink the convoy!

At 9 am, JU 87 'Stukas' of StG 1, 2 and 77 were over 'Peewit'. They were escorted by 109s from JG 27 under the command of Major Max Ibel and were being plotted by the Ventnor radar station. Together with other squadrons from No. 11 Group and one from No. 10, 145 Squadron engaged the enemy over the convoy causing the Germans to break up their systematic dropping of bombs on the ships. In this particular fight three Stukas were shot down with six badly damaged and several of the escorting fighters were also shot down. The attack had however sunk four more ships in the convoy leaving several more with further damage.

The attacks were resumed at 12.45 am by a further force of Stukas from Fliegerkorps VIII who arrived over the convoy just as 145 were refuelling and rearming at Westhampnett. Shouting to his pilots to get airborne with what they had on board, Sqd.Ldr J R A Peel, the CO, led 145 back into the fray. Climbing to 16,000 ft, he led his pilots out of the sun as they literally fell upon the pack of enemy aircraft. In seconds the sky was full of twisting, turning, snarling metal as the two forces became locked in combat. Several enemy aircraft were seen to crash very near the convoy which was still moving towards the shelter of Weymouth Bay. Together with 43 Squadron from Tangmere, 145 sent a number of the Luftwaffe to the bottom of the sea but not without loss to themselves. As nightfall came and the remaining four ships of the convoy limped into Swanage harbour, 145 mourned their dead. Five Hurricanes plus their pilots had been lost. Sgt. E D Baker, P/Os L A Sears, E C J Wakeham, F/O Lord R U P Kay-Shuttleworth and Sub-Lieutenant F A Smith of the Fleet Air Arm were missing presumed dead. The claims for both sides were once again exaggerated with the Luftwaffe claiming 45 Spitfires and Hurricanes lost, the actual number being 17 and Fighter Command claiming 55, the number eventually being 26. 145 Squadron was the top scoring unit.

As congratulatory telegrams arrived for Flt.Lt. Adrian Boyd (5 kills), Sqd.Ldr. John Peel, Flt. Lt. Roy Dutton and P/O Weir (3 kills each), the squadron felt no urge to celebrate as they remembered their fallen colleagues. An evening visit by the Secretary of State for Air, the Chief of the Air Staff and Air Vice Marshal Dowding himself did little to dispel their gloom. Later a visit by HRH the Duke of Gloucester to congratulate them for their magnificent achievement still left them empty and not at all appreciative of the gesture. Though it was a bad day for 145, the Luftwaffe had suffered even more because they had put in the greatest effort of the war so far and many did not return home to Germany that night.

Three days later 145 were once again in trouble as heavy attacks by the enemy developed over the Portland area. By 9.30 am the Ventnor radar station had picked up a large enemy force heading for Weymouth. David Lloyd, the sector controller, scrambled 12 Hurricanes from 145 together with six other squadrons from 11 Group. They found 150 bombers, mostly JU 88s and HE IIIs escorted by ME 109s and 110s and immediately tore into the heart of them. It was almost a repeat of 8th August as four Hurricanes fell from the sky. F/O G R Branch and F/O A Ostowicz were killed and Sqd.Ldr. Peel and P/O Weir managed to force land their stricken aircraft. The next day, Monday 12th August also saw the squadron lose four Hurricanes with the loss of three more pilots. In a case of mistaken identity, a Spitfire was suspected of having fired on Hurricane P3736 causing the aircraft to crash at Westhampnett. The pilot Flt.Lt. A H McN Boyd escaped unhurt.

Tuesday 13th August saw 'Eagle Day' dawn with early morning

mist and drizzle in places. Due to the weather, the main thrust of the German attacks did not materialise until after midday. 145 were not scrambled that day as the remnants of the squadron were preparing to move away from the battle front and they took their remaining Hurricanes to Drem in Scotland the next day. For them Westhampnett had seen great success but it also had brought them great sorrow. They were not sorry to leave. No. 602 (City of Glasgow) Squadron of the Royal Auxiliary Air Force flew their Spitfires to the airfield on the 13th and were soon settling into the routine of a front-line satellite airfield after their days of frustration at Drem. The first scramble occurred the next day at 6.50 am and their first blood came shortly after as they flew over the Isle of Wight and sent the German early reconnaissance DO 17 to the bottom of the Channel.

The 16th saw very heavy attacks including one on Tangmere, the mother airfield. With the weather mainly fair and warm and a slight Channel haze, the first raids were coming over by 11 am. The targets were the Kent airfields, Norfolk and outer London with a big raid over Portland just after midday. As the raid split, sections arrived over Ventnor and Tangmere. 602 went to the defence of Tangmere as the Stukas escorted by 109s attempted to wipe Tangmere from the map. Only two Spitfires were damaged with the pilots surviving and three hours later 602 were scrambled once again, this time successfully downing 2 ME 110s of ZG 76 operating from Stavanger in Norway.

Two days later the Luftwaffe attacked Gosport, Thorney Island and Ford airfields and 602 were in action shortly after midday. This time they suffered one Spitfire lost and four damaged. F/O C J Mounts' Spitfire was badly mauled by 109s but he managed to land at nearby Ford with damage to his engine. Although he landed safely, a burst tyre as he did so caused his Spitfire to nose over. He did however manage to walk away, cursing as he did so! Spitfire K9969 flown by F/O P Ferguson fared the worst, for after being hit in the port wing and petrol tank, the aircraft was further damaged when it collided with the Poling RDF mast and again when it flew through HT cables as it was about to crash land. F/O Ferguson lived to fly another day although he was badly wounded and suffering from shock. Flt.Lt. J D Urie landed his damaged Spitfire back at base although badly wounded and Sgt. E Whall ditched his aircraft at Elmer Sands, Middleton and walked away unhurt. The only radar station hit and put out of action in this raid was Poling and it was suggested that F/O Ferguson did more damage to it than the Luftwaffe had! The day was significant because it brought the end to Stuka operations over mainland Britain. The losses to the aircraft were quite unacceptable even to Goering. Fighter Command flying 766 sorties and together with the Ack-ack had accounted for 71 enemy aircraft. 27 RAF fighters had been lost with ten pilots killed, and it was this loss of pilots that worried Dowding. The training units were now passing out pilots in two weeks instead of the usual four, with the result that the men were still relatively inexperienced and very soon tired after long periods of aerial fighting. They were sent for rest periods but the replacements suffered from the same fatigue and not surprisingly many of them never saw the week out.

The next day, yet again P/O Moody was forced to bale out of his blazing Spitfire after being fired upon by a JU 88 off Bognor. He landed just outside Arundel with severe burns to his hands as 602 flew over him to land back at Westhampnett, refuel , rearm and be scrambled again within minutes.

The rest of August continued in similar vein as the Luftwaffe continued its onslaught. The 26th August saw three major attacks by large formations. The late morning and early afternoon saw raids on the Kent airfields with a major raid on Portsmouth and Southampton developing at 4 pm by KG 55. In fierce combat over the Isle of Wight, the 109s of JG 2 and 3 suffered badly, together with the DO 17s of KG 2 and 55. As the enemy came in low over Portsmouth, shoppers in the busy town either ran for the shelters or just looked up at the enemy. Children, too young to really know fear, resisted the tug of their parents to get them to safety. To them it was all a game. As the raids continued to the end of the month, it was a miracle how the RAF continued to battle with the enemy.

The 1st September saw a Fighter Command diarist (usually one of the most junior airmen) record: 'Dowding's forces are now suffering from accumulated fatigue and the mounting losses in pilots.' As the month broke fine and warm there was certainly no indication that the present tactics of the enemy against the airfields would change. The first few days of the month saw a continuation of the same as Hitler became impatient at the delay in clearing the RAF from the sky. On the night of 25th/26th August, Bomber Command had carried out a retaliatory raid on Berlin. This so enraged Hitler that he ordered

Sergeant C F Babbage was fortunately rescued by fishermen after his Spitfire was shot down. He survived several similar incidents and was awarded the DFM for his successes against the enemy (Worthing Library).

Goering to concentrate his attacks on London and the larger cities. This change of tactics saved the airfields of No. 11 Group from total destruction though at the expense of civilian lives.

On 7th September, the bombing switched to London and on the same day 602 lost two of its pilots. 23 year old P/O W H Coverley, badly burnt, baled out of his blazing Spitfire over Tonbridge and died where he landed, his body lying undiscovered for nine days. Of P/O Moody, who had survived being shot down on 19th August, no trace was ever found. He is remembered along with 537 other airmen on the Runnymede Memorial.

With the change in tactics by the Luftwaffe, 602 undertook night flying training in order to catch the enemy by night. Though they became very proficient in theory, the practice of using the Spitfire in this rôle proved a total failure. The squadron still undertook the day defence rôle, 11th September proving a particularly bad day when 602 lost three aircraft together with one pilot, Sgt. Mervyn Sprague during a skirmish with ME 109s and 110s over Selsey Bill. The day was significant however as Hitler issued orders that 'Sealion', the

British parents were not alone in mourning their sons. A youthful member of the crew of a JU 88, Gefr. Petermann, died when his plane was shot down into the sea in 1940. He was given a military funeral (Worthing Library).

planned invasion of Britain, was to be postponed until at least the 24th. That too was dependent on the Luftwaffe gaining aerial supremacy over this country.

As the nightly raids on the cities continued, the attacks on the airfields became less. 602 was still meeting the enemy frequently, the 27th being memorable to Sgt C F Babbage who was shot down for the third time in less than four weeks. He led a charmed life for he remained unhurt in all three incidents. 'Sealion' did not take place on the 24th, Hitler once again postponing the invasion. The end of the month and early October did however bring a new tactic into use as bomb carrying ME 109s and 110s came over. Each Gruppe of fighter/ bombers was provided with an escort of fighters making it a formidable force.

October saw the fifth and final phase of the Battle of Britain and 602 played a very significant part in it. Germany had certainly not gained the air superiority that it needed and the fighter/bomber operations increased. Throughout October 602 carried on the fight. On the 12th,

Sergeant Babbage once again defied death as his damaged Spitfire turned over during a forced landing at Lewes but the month as a whole saw only eight aircraft losses for 602 with seven pilots safe. By the 31st the Battle of Britain was deemed to be over as the nights began to draw in, but the nightly raids continued and intensified. The Battle had taken its toll of 1,733 enemy aircraft for the loss of 915 of Fighter Command but both forces had lost men in the flower of their youth. Winston Churchill immortalised the RAF in his speech to the country stating: 'Never in the field of human conflict was so much owed by so many to so few.'

602 were joined on 23rd November 1940 by No. 302 Polish Squadron which had adopted the regional title 'Poznam' from their homeland. They had formed at Leconfield on 13th July 1940 with Polish personnel who had escaped from France after the German invasion. They came in their Hurricanes from Northolt, where they had flown during the final stages of the Battle.

602 remained at Westhampnett until 17th December 1940 when they were posted to Prestwick. They had given their all during their stay and at no time were they sent for rest periods, the airfield had remained their home throughout that long hot summer. Farewell Westhampnett, you made us men! To replace them came 610 (County of Chester) Squadron, Royal Auxiliary Air Force with Spitfires making the satellite a two squadron station. It remained this way over Christmas 1940 and into the New Year. The snowy weather caused further waterlogging at the airfield and this prompted the decision to build a hard perimeter track around the field. Dispersal areas also became hardstanding and the airmen's accommodation was upgraded together with several Blister hangars to ensure the maintenance and repair of the aircraft was no longer carried out in the open.

And so Westhampnett entered the second year of the war with 302 and 610 Squadrons in residence. January saw 302 flying some standing patrols along the south coast whilst 610 had undertaken the occasional 'Circus' operation, a duty entailing bomber escort with a view to enticing the enemy to appear. These were the first of the offensive operations to be carried out by Fighter Command which gradually increased as the Allies began the long fight back.

With the arrival of spring and the better weather, more thought was given to operations across the Channel and as the Poles of 302 took their Hurricanes to Kenley in April, 616 (South Yorkshire) Squadron flew the short hop from Tangmere to Westhampnett. They had arrived to form part of the Tangmere wing of Spitfires which comprised 610 and 616 Squadrons at Westhampnett and 145 Squadron at another satellite of Tangmere named Merston. The wing was to be commanded by the legendary Douglas Bader who chose to lead the wing flying in the ranks of 616 Squadron. Upon his arrival at Tangmere, one of the first comments he made was the fact that the two white runways shone like beacons on moonlit nights, a permanent landmark for the German bombers flying overhead. Though he suggested to the Air Ministry that they be camouflaged, no notice was taken until Bader himself brought it to the notice of the *Sunday Express*. The resulting publicity, although putting Bader in the Ministry's bad books, had the desired effect, and hastily the runways of Tangmere were camouflaged with paint. Though only a grass airfield, Westhampnett also received a degree of camouflage which had the intended effect of confusing the enemy.

By April the terrifying night raids by the Germans were becoming

The Tangmere Wing of Spitfires flew from Westhampnett during 1941, commanded by the indomitable Douglas Bader, seen in the centre of the photograph (A Saunders Collection).

less and the war seemed to be a little slow after the hectic past year. It was time for Fighter Command to take the initiative and go over fully to the offensive. The first operation took place on 17th April when 100 Spitfires of Fighter Command escorted 12 Blenheims on a bombing mission to Cherbourg. Thirty-six of the aircraft belonged to the Tangmere wing but the mission proved 'a piece of cake' without any sign of the enemy. Several more missions produced similar results until 8th May when four aircraft of the wing including two from 610 Squadron, carried out a 'taunting' mission along the French coast. Sure enough they were jumped by five ME 109s. Cocky Dundas, flying as No. 2 to Bader called urgently, 'Hello Dogsbody [Bader's call sign]. Five 109s five o' clock above.' 'Oh good' replied Bader, 'I can see them. Oh, this is just what we wanted isn't it?' The 109s came in for the kill as four Spitfires spun round on their wingtips. Two Spitfires were hit by enemy fire but all four managed to get home safely. One of the enemy was sent down in flames and two were damaged. Over the coming weeks the wing perfected the 'Circus and Rhubarb' techniques and encountered many skirmishes with the enemy.

With this increase in personnel at Westhampnett, extra accommodation had to be found. Whilst the officers still used Shopwyke Hall as their mess, many were sleeping out at a large rambling house called Rushmans. For a satellite airfield, Westhampnett was becoming extremely crowded and when in July both squadrons converted from their Spitfire IIs to VBs, they were further strengthened by more personnel. In addition to the usual escort duties, the wing was also carrying out low level strike operations against any target in occupied Europe. Daily the wing came into contact with ME 109s and daily, Douglas Bader insisted on leading the wing, always flying with 616 Squadron. At one period he did ten sweeps in seven days, enough to give the average pilot severe fatigue yet still he refused to take a rest period, even against the advice of the Air Officer Commanding, Leigh-Mallory himself. On 8th August, when his eyes were beginning to show signs of strain, it was arranged for him and his wife together with a colleague to take a spell of rest in Scotland. Bader agreed but only if he could lead one more sweep. The next day a 'Circus' was planned with Douglas leading the wing. That very morning everything went wrong!

616 took off from Westhampnett and crossed the French coast at Le

Touquet. Flying at 28/30,000 ft to enable the wing to fly out of the sun at the enemy Douglas saw a dozen 109s below them. 'Dogsbody attacking. Plenty for all.' The wing dived and at 24,000 ft Douglas aimed at the leading aircraft and gave a three second burst. Bits flew off and glycol began streaming from its engine as it went into a dive. Noticing two other 109s turning towards him, Douglas turned right when something hit him. He had collided with an enemy aircraft. The Spitfire lurched as he pulled the stick back into his stomach. Nothing happened and his aircraft continued diving. Looking behind he saw he was missing his tail fin, it had all gone. He realised that his Spitfire was mortally wounded and that he must bale out or die. He pulled off his mask, undid his harness and released his cockpit canopy. Pulling himself out of the seat with great difficulty, he felt the slipstream tearing at his face. He pulled and pulled but could not free himself from the cockpit. He looked down and through painfully half closed eyes, saw that his artificial right leg was trapped beneath the rudder pedals. Gaining the strength of a person possessed as his aircraft plunged towards earth, he suddenly fell out of the cockpit. Watching his beloved aircraft fall away beneath him, he pulled the ripcord of his parachute and with satisfaction, felt the jolt as it opened. Looking down he saw the raw white stump of his right leg and realised that the leg was still in the aircraft.

The rest of the wing returned to base and could not believe that Douglas had not returned. No-one had seen him go down and it was not until some time later that the Germans informed Fighter Command that he was indeed safe and a prisoner at St Omer airfield. It was arranged that a replacement leg be sent to him and on 19th August during a 'Circus' operation by 616 Squadron, a parcel containing a new leg was dropped to him. The rest of his escapades whilst a prisoner of the Third Reich is history!

On 29th August 1941, 610 Squadron moved to Leconfield, followed in October by 616 who took their Spitfire VBs to Kirton-in-Lindsey. To replace 610 came 120 (Mysore) Squadron also with Spitfire VBs. This was one of the named Indian squadrons, the crest incorporating the Indian insignia of the Gunda Bherunda of Mysore. They left on detachment to Debden in November but were back at Westhampnett by 23rd December 1941. Another named unit, No. 65 (East India) Squadron flew their VBs in from Kirton-in-Lindsey on 7th October and both squadrons carried out 'Rhubarbs' over occupied Europe.

With Christmas fast approaching, 65 left for Debden as No. 41 flew over from Merston, another satellite of Tangmere, to make Westhampnett their home until Spring 1942. The lead up to Christmas involved both squadrons in offensive operations, 129 clashing with several ME 109s during one operation claiming three destroyed, three probables and four damaged for the loss of three aircraft and two pilots.

With the war now going very much in the Allies favour, there was much talk of just how much longer it would continue. Christmas was celebrated as much as was possible while the relentless offensive against enemy occupied territory continued. With the opening of the Russian campaign in June 1941, much of the Luftwaffe's striking power had been diverted from Europe for this purpose. However, by Spring 1942, when an enormous raid by Bomber Command on Lubeck aroused fury in the German High Command, Hitler ordered that the air war against the British was to be vigorously renewed with large attacks against the smaller cities. By this time however, the British night defences had greatly improved since those dark days in 1940 and the night-fighters were having great success.

For Westhampnett, April 1942 saw 41 Squadron return to Merston and for two days in July, No. 340 (Ile-de-France) Squadron of the Free French used the base. When they left for Hornchurch, 129 were still carrying out offensive patrols over Northern France until their departure on 30th July to nearby Thorney Island. At this stage, Westhampnett entered a new era when it became United States Army Air Force base 352 and the home of the 31st Fighter Group with Spitfires. The airfield still came under the care and control of Tangmere but for the local populace of Chichester and the surrounding district, it was a case of 'lock up your daughters' as the Americans flooded into the towns in the evenings. They began flying operations immediately upon arrival with convoy escort and 'Rhubarbs' over France.

As the date set for 'Operation Jubilee', the Dieppe raid, approached, Westhampnett in common with all the No. 11 Group airfields became closed to all but essential personnel. The task of the USAAF in Britain during this period was to provide cover throughout the day, to attack enemy coast defences and batteries and to lay a smoke cover over the east headland during the assault and withdrawal. Indeed at the end of the ill-fated operation, one of the

The memorial plaque to the 31st Fighter Group of the USAAF who flew from Westhampnett – doubtless to the delight of local girls – in 1942 (R J Brooks).

outstanding features was the high degree of protection afforded to both the Fleet and the troops on shore by the RAF and the USAAF.

At his headquarters at No. 11 Group, Air Marshall Leigh-Mallory took personal charge of the flying operations. He had 56 squadrons of fighters and 11 squadrons of light bombers together with several of reconnaissance Mustangs at his disposal, all of which took part at some time in the operation. As dusk fell on 19th August, almost 3,000 sorties had been flown. Although the Dieppe operation resulted in a terrible loss of life, the protecting fighters had done their job admirably.

The rest of August saw the 308th FS at Westhampnett and a visit on the 2nd September from General Carl Spaatz, the CO of the 8th Air Force, brought them under the umbrella of the 12th Air Force, although they continued to work under the auspices of No. 11 Group Fighter Command. By October they had gone and the airfield reverted fully to a satellite of Tangmere with the arrival of 616 Squadron, many of the pilots remembering the days of flying with the Tangmere wing under the leadership of Douglas Bader. They commenced 'Rhubarb' operations with the new Spitfire VIs and later in the month began day bomber escort sweeps more commonly known as 'Ramrods'. They were joined on 7th November 1942 by No. 131 (County of Kent) Squadron. This was another of the named squadrons, in this instance in recognition of the fact that the people of Kent had collected money by various means to enable the purchase of several Spitfires, but although the Air Ministry chose to name the squadron after the county they never flew from a Kentish airfield. The Spitfire VBs flew across from Thorney Island and had settled into Westhampnett by nightfall. Like 616 they carried out 'Rhubarbs and Ramrods', clashing frequently with the enemy and gaining a fair amount of success.

The operations continued over the New Year of 1943 before it became all change at the airfield with the departure of 616 and 131 Squadrons and the arrival of Nos. 485 (RNZAF) and 610, the latter County of Chester Squadron having flown from Westhampnett just after the Battle of Britain. On 30th January 1943, no doubt the German people and the German High Command celebrated the 10th anniversary of Hitler's rise to power. It must have been a very hollow celebration as Stalingrad fell to the Russians. This together with the victories at El Alamein and the landings in North Africa marked the turning point of the war against Germany. Though still a long way off, victory was in sight.

The relentless pounding of occupied Europe continued as all of the south and south east coastal airfields carried the war back to the enemy. The squadrons also constantly tangled with ME 109s and FW 190s that came across the Channel on hit and run raids on coastal towns. 501 (County of Gloucester) Squadron flew in from Bally-halbert with their Spitfire VCs on 30th April and were joined by 167 (Gold Coast) Squadron on 21st May. Westhampnett was now experiencing a rapid change of units as the summer saw 41 Squadron return for the first time since 1941, and 91 (Nigeria) Squadron arrived with Spitfire XIIs from Hawkinge.

The wing continued on the offensive and with several large scale dogfights taking place, the month of September resulted in 41 Squadron being the top scorer in Fighter Command. The Wing moved to Tangmere in October and were replaced on the 10th of the month by 174, 175 and 245 Squadrons. They combined to form 121

Airfield and had previously been based at the Advanced Landing Ground at Lydd in Kent. The local populace were once again upset at the sound of their Typhoon 1Bs, as civilians were wherever that particular type of aircraft operated. Since 1942 the Typhoon had carried 250 lb bombs beneath the wings and this was the type of operation flown by the squadrons during their stay at Westhampnett. All three squadrons operated throughout the autumn of 1943 against enemy shipping as part of the 'Channel Stop' campaign. They also took part in offensive sweeps over France, Belgium and Holland. The aircraft had become famous for its 'train busting' operations and by the end of 1943, as many as 150 trains were being destroyed each month by Typhoons of various squadrons, bringing havoc to the German supply lines.

Late 1943 and early 1944 saw the build-up to the invasion of Europe and command of the Allied Tactical Air Forces was given to Air Chief-Marshal Sir Trafford Leigh-Mallory. He gathered together a very formidable force to provide cover for the troops and to carry out preliminary bombing of the area. The Allies devised a deception plan codenamed 'Bodyguard' to give the impression that the landings were to be in the region of the Pas-de-Calais. The success of this plan was helped by Hitler himself who was convinced that any landing in Europe would use the shortest sea crossing, ie Dover, to the Pas-de-Calais. Dawn on 6th June 1944 however proved Hitler wrong.

In preparation for 'Operation Overlord', Westhampnett saw a succession of squadrons arrive and depart. On 1st April, 121 Airfield moved out to be replaced by 144 Airfield comprising Nos. 441 (Silver Fox), 442 (Caribou) and 443 (Hornet) squadrons of the Royal Canadian Air Force, all flying Spitfire IXBs. They arrived mainly to complete a training programme connected with the assault but also carried out escort sweeps to bombers. Their training completed, they left for Funtington on 24th April. Westhampnett now became home to 129 Airfield with just one squadron, No. 184. Once again the Typhoon returned, to the dismay of the locals, and with a detachment to Holmsley South for six days they were back at the airfield for D Day. They joined No. 84 Group Communications Squadron and as dawn broke on 6th June, the Typhoons roared away from Westhampnett to be one of the first squadrons over the assault area. Conditions were reasonable despite a gloomy forecast. As the pilots of 184 looked down upon the mass of shipping below, they saw the fighter direction ship which was to be used to control the air forces, but for the early morning flyers the controller on board had nothing. 184 carried out about four sorties on that fateful day, not once did they see the enemy. It was all very disappointing, for the pilots knew that it could very well be the last chance for large scale contact with the enemy. Despite this it was obvious that the Allied air forces had dominance in the air and 184 had done a good job in attacking ground targets with their rockets.

The next day saw 184 in action once again and with the Allies now firmly established in Europe, Westhampnett was earmarked as a forward airfield in support of the push towards Berlin. It was intended that the airfield should become a Mosquito base but due to the lack of runway lighting and the fact that the Mosquito needed a

Today Westhampnett is again used for flying. Among other original RAF buildings is the Watch Office (R.J. Brooks).

121

fairly long runway, the idea was abandoned and instead it became an anti-diver airfield.

184 Squadron moved to Holmsley South on 17th June to allow the Spitfire XIIs of 41 Squadron to return together with the XIVs of 610 Squadron. They only carried out a few V1 interceptions before moving to Friston, just a short distance away from Westhampnett, to continue 'Diver' operations. Beachhead patrols and bomber escorts were then flown from the airfield by Nos. 13, 303 (Polish) and 402 (RCAF) squadrons. They marked the beginning of a three month period of extensive escort operations flown by short stay squadrons. By the end of September the Spitfires had left and throughout October, no flying was done from Westhampnett as the main theatre of the war was now over Europe. No. 83 Group Support Unit arrived during November with mainly Spitfires and Mustangs. The airfield was now used as a ferry base from which replacement aircraft were flown to the units operating across the continent, but with the transfer of the GSU to Dunsfold on 22nd February 1945, Westhampnett went into care and maintenance.

With increased pressure being placed upon the parent station of Tangmere, the Naval Air Fighting Development Unit moved to Westhampnett in July 1945, just prior to the end of the war. The airfield was reactivated but with the cessation of hostilities, the new lease of life could not be sustained. The end came quietly and quickly on the 13th May 1946.

After its years as a racing circuit the former Westhampnett is once again used for flying, and today Goodwood sees over 50,000 aircraft movements a year, this is set to increase as the popularity of this satellite airfield to Tangmere grows.

6
SHOREHAM

Apart from the years 1918-1921 the grass airfield of Shoreham was used for civilian aviation (see Chapter One) until the distant rumblings from Germany brought a new and intense turn of fortunes.

For some time it had been appreciated that the international situation was deteriorating and it was this deterioration that plagued the hopes for growth at Shoreham. The years of 1936 and 1937 saw a big expansion of the RAF. Many civilian flying organisations were only too willing to accept military contracts to carry out flying training for potential pilots and the recently arrived Martin School of Air Navigation at Shoreham did just that. They received an RAF Volunteer Reserve Pilot Training contract on 1st July 1937. Known as No. 16 Elementary and Reserve Flying Training School, it was initially equipped with Tiger Moths and later joined by Hawker Harts and Hinds. Wooden huts sprang up around the perimeter of the airfield for the trainees, these being used both as classrooms and accommodation. The school was further enlarged in 1937 with the addition of a bombing navigation course. Both schools survived until late August 1939 when, with war very imminent, No. 16 E & RFTS moved out. The airfield however was to continue its civilian usage for the rest of 1939 and the early part of 1940.

When the Battle of Britain began, life still carried on very much the same but with the air battles overhead growing in size and frequency, June 1940 saw a stop to civilian flying and Shoreham prepared for war.

The airfield was designated as an advanced airfield in the Kenley

123

Balloon barrages such as this impressive display over Sussex became an increasingly familiar wartime sight and gave some measure of confidence to beleaguered cities (South Eastern Newspapers).

Sector of No. 11 Group Fighter Command. Throughout June the field remained empty despite the fierce battles going on above. Its first real use came in the middle of July when a detachment of Westland Lysander IIs arrived from Tilshead. They were part of 225 Squadron who also had detachments at Okehampton, Pembrey, Exeter and Staverton. The aircraft were used for flying coastal patrols along the coasts of Sussex, Hampshire and the Isle of Wight and these were interspersed with the occasional Air Sea Rescue duties and some Army Co-operation work.

Just a short distance away, Tangmere was suffering at the hands of the German bombers. With the airfield barely usable, the Fighter Interception Unit left and flew the short distance to Shoreham equipped with Beaufighters. The grass of Shoreham proved most unsuitable for this heavy aircraft and little work was carried out by the unit for some time. The FIU were joined on 14th October 1940 by No. 422 Flight with Hurricanes which were used in the night-fighting rôle. The Hurricane was primarily a day fighter, but late in 1940 and early 1941 was the period when the specialist night-fighter squadrons with their own twin engined Beaufighters were only just being formed. Faced with the predicament of constant night attacks by the Germans, the Air Ministry pressed single engined day fighters into

124

service as night-fighters. Initially the Mk. I Hurricane was used but by 1941 the new Mk. IIC was the variant most widely employed for this type of operation. No. 422 Flight were amongst the forerunners of Hurricane night-fighting and achieved a modest success whilst at Shoreham.

The Flight moved to Cranage in January 1941 followed shortly after by the FIU. Further extensions took place at the airfield and with the Luftwaffe carrying out a series of hit and run raids during July and August, it was not until 25th October that another unit formed at Shoreham in the shape of No. 11 Group Target Towing Flight with Westland Lysanders. The aircraft were used to pull drogue targets for fighter squadrons to get air-firing experience. The Flight was allocated six aircraft which became No. 1488 TT Flight on 1st December 1941. They carried out sterling work as target tugs, not really the best of flying duties and very unexciting work. Two more Lysanders arrived at Shoreham for ASR work and in December formed 'C' Flight of No. 277 Squadron. With detachments at Martle-

Hitler's 'Eagle Day' in August 1940 was not the success he had hoped for. Many German aircraft were lost during air battles over the south coast, including that of Oberleutnant Paul Temme, who was taken prisoner after his ME 109E-1 was shot down near Shoreham airfield (A Saunders Collection).

sham Heath and Hawkinge (see *Kent Airfields Remembered*), in addition to the Lysanders they also used the Supermarine Walrus, known affectionately to all flying men as the 'Shagbat'. Originally designed to be catapulted from warships, it came into its own when used on ASR duties and many pilots after being shot down in the sea were to owe their lives to the Walrus. 277 rescued many airmen from the cold waters of the Channel during late 1941 and early 1942. No other resident squadrons were based at this grass airfield during this period and in fact it seemed as though Shoreham had been forgotten. Nearby Tangmere, Westhampnett and even Thorney Island were certainly in the thick of the fighting but all three airfields had reason to be grateful to the courage and devotion of 277 Squadron.

A detachment of 245 Squadron with Hurricane IIBs flew in on 19th December and as 1941 passed into history, the New Year brought little change until 24th May when 253 Squadron flew their Hurricanes in for a stay lasting six days. They departed to Hibaldstow on the 30th and with the date set for 'Operation Jubilee', the ill fated Dieppe raid, No. 3 Squadron also flew their Hurricane IICs in from Hunsdon and the 245 Squadron detachment returned. The stage was set for the assault that became known as the blackest day in Canadian military history.

Both units were in action early on 19th August 1942 as they were scrambled to accompany No. 43 Squadron from Tangmere on the first fighter sweep. For the Shoreham based Hurricanes it was a disaster as two collided on the ground prior to take-off. The rest of the aircraft flew across the Channel in company with 43 and began to attack the enemy gun positions overlooking the beach. The enemy gunfire proved very accurate as one of 43's Hurricanes was shot down followed by three of 245 Squadron. The remainder of the aircraft returned to Tangmere and Shoreham respectively and were immediately refuelled and rearmed before making their second crossing of the Channel. Once again the aircraft came under heavy fire and several were lost. Some returned to Shoreham badly damaged and it was many a cursing airman who patched them up ready for another sortie! As twilight descended on that epic day, the squadrons at Shoreham counted the cost. The Dieppe raid had been equally disastrous for the RAF, 245 Squadron were left with just three usable aircraft whilst No. 3, although faring a little better, had also lost valuable aircraft and pilots. By 20th August the two squadrons had

The Supermarine Sea Otter replaced the Walrus as a more effective means of air-sea rescue. Many a downed airman struggling in the sea was relieved at the appearance of such an aircraft (MAP).

departed and once again Shoreham was left with 277 Squadron. The ASR Flight received Boulton Paul Defiants to replace the Lysanders in May 1942. It still retained the faithful Walrus which earned the pilot, Sergeant T Fletchers and his gunner, Sergeant L Healey, the DFM apiece when they picked up a downed airman from right under the German guns at Cap Gris Nez.

On 25th November, the airfield changed from an ALG of Kenley to a satellite of Ford, an airfield just a short distance away. The year ended with little change at the airfield but the New Year saw the heaviest attack by the Luftwaffe which caused widespread damage. It was of little value to the enemy for it still only contained the ASR Flight.

1943 also continued with little change. 277 Squadron were still resident though in February they converted from the Defiant to Spitfire IIs, still retaining the Walrus for the actual pick-ups. Shoreham became No. 7 AA Practice Camp in April with the arrival of many would-be RAF Regiment gunners. Once again the Westland Lysander returned to the airfield to act as target tug, and in August the unit received the title of No. 1631 Flight. The number of personnel increased during the year as the regiment became a very important part of the RAF, and the Lysanders were a familiar sight along the Sussex coast trailing their target drogues. The regiment strength increased once again when No. 18 Armament Practice Camp formed at Shoreham in October. The Lysander Flight was amalgamated with No. 1622 at Gosport to form 667 Squadron of which C Flight returned to Shoreham, once again equipped with Defiants. With this intense period of training, a gunnery training dome was built on the northern perimeter of the airfield. Constructed of concrete slabs, it served as an instructional classroom and was of such solid foundation that it survives today.

Since its beginning, Shoreham had been a grass airfield. During the autumn and winter the grass became so sodden that it rendered the airfield unserviceable for long periods. This was partially rectified in February 1944 when a metal track strip, similar to Sommerfeld Track, was laid along the 03/21 runway. This improved the all weather use of the airfield although heavy aircraft would often rip sections of it up. It was however a great improvement.

In March, Shoreham became a forward satellite to Tangmere and 277 Squadron exchanged their Walrus for a Supermarine Sea Otter. This, the last of a long line of biplane amphibious aircraft, had twice the range of the Walrus and was aerodynamically and hydrodynamically superior. Made by Saunders Roe under licence, it too became a firm favourite with the ASR Squadrons. 277 moved its headquarters from Gravesend to Shoreham on 15th April 1944, an indication of the importance that was placed on Shoreham. April also saw the arrival of the airfield's first Spitfires, when No. 345 (Free French) Squadron flew their Spitfire VBs from Ayr. The squadron had been formed on 12th February 1944 and comprised French personnel transferred from North Africa.

Shoreham was about to enter the busiest military period of its whole career as 345 began operations on 2nd May. They formed part of No. 141 Wing of the 2nd Tactical Air Force and flew many patrols over the Normandy beach-heads. In addition, 'Ramrods' were flown frequently with Free French Light Bomber Squadrons operating from Hartford Bridge. Contact with the enemy was frequent and 345 found a lot of success. As June approached, preparations were well advanced for the greatest amphibious assault of the war. It was known as 'Operation Overlord'. The assault was intended to drive

Another means of rescuing pilots from the sea was the high speed launch, such as this HSL 127 leaving harbour (South Eastern Newspapers).

the Germans out of France and the Low Countries and was scheduled to begin at dawn on 6th June – D Day. 345 were briefed to carry out beach and convoy patrols prior to this date, and in preparation for the big day a visit by General P J Koenig, the Commander of the Free French Forces, was arranged.

The 6th dawned mistily as 345 were briefed on the day's operations. They were off on the first mission by 9 am and witnessed the scene below as the Allied invasion began. Later in the day they escorted the glider formations that were being towed to the assault area, coming into contact once again with the Luftwaffe but losing several aircraft in the process. The next two days were spent covering the invasion area and then it was back to the usual operations. No. 345 left Shoreham on the 16th August 1944 and moved over to the ALG at Deanland. The airfield reverted to the status of a satellite and except for the operations of 277 Squadron, remained very quiet.

And so it stayed until late 1944. Although war was to rage on for a further eight months, the airfield saw very little use. The station headquarters closed in September for as aircraft became heavier and faster, the grass airfield was of no use. 277 took their aircraft to Hawkinge in October and Shoreham went into care and maintenance. It had not realised anything like its true potential, the one handicap being that it remained a grass airfield. After the war it resumed life as an important civil airfield.

Today there is still visible evidence of the past years of the airfield. Dotted around the perimeter are various air-raid shelters and concrete gun emplacements. Lying in the grass are two Pickett-Hamilton retractable gun forts but standing supreme and overlooking all of this is the superb gunnery training dome on the northern perimeter. Still in fair condition, it is a unique building for no other airfield in the South of England has one. It is hoped that it will be preserved and become a listed building.

The return of the King's Cup Air Race to the airfield in 1985 was a sign of faith by the aviation world for Shoreham is a very fine example of how a municipal airport should be run. At the time of writing, there are plans to reintroduce a Channel Islands service and with this possibility, the future of Shoreham is virtually assured.

7
FRISTON

The Civil Defence War Diaries for East Sussex recorded the following incidents relating to Friston airfield:

9-7-42   06.00hrs Two high explosive bombs on Friston also machine gunning – unspecified number wounded. EA [enemy aircraft] flew over Birling then out to sea.

9-8-42   Clocks went back one hour. 23.04hrs Over 2,000 lbs dropped in Portslade area of which 15% were UXBs [unexploded bombs]. HE also dropped near Friston at 23.05hrs. 23.45hrs HE dropped on Friston.

6-12-42   22.35hrs. EA shot down in flames onto Friston. 22.45hrs HE dropped on Friston.

21-1-43   ? JU 88 flew over Friston towards East Dean. Five enemy aircraft engaged by AA. Friston airfield badly hit with six killed, three injured and 18 slightly injured. Phones out of use for 45 mins.

For an emergency landing ground Friston attracted a lot of attention from enemy aircraft but this was mainly due to its prominent position on top of the Seven Sisters cliffs, just five miles west of Eastbourne. This position also ensured that it was the first airfield badly damaged aircraft saw when returning from raids on enemy occupied Europe. Hence, Friston was usually to be found with many different types parked around its perimeter in various stages of distress. It was for its size and very unusual shape, an extremely busy airfield.

Though subject to scrutiny, it is firmly believed that the site, owned by the Church Commissioners, was first used in the 1930s as a place of aviation by Mr Victor Yates of Eastbourne who owned the motor works and garage at Cavendish Place in the town. It is further rumoured that he was the first man in Eastbourne and possibly the whole of Sussex, to design and construct an aeroplane. Having previously flown at Brooklands and Hendon, he chose Friston to carry on with his experiments after gaining the permission of the Church. Sited on ground adjoining Link Farm and Exceat Farm, it was a fairly level piece of grass in the shape of a V. The shape however did not deter the Directorate of Public Works from looking at the site seriously during the rapid expansion period of 1939/40.

Its first military use however came during 1936 when it was used as a training ground by Nos. 2 and 4 Squadrons operating from Hawkinge and Odiham respectively. It was also an excuse for a very pleasant flight and a day sunning the body whilst perched high up on the cliffs! Sometimes referred to as Gayles or East Dean, the airfield's use as a training base was very brief and Friston lay deserted from 1938 until the summer of 1940 when No. 11 Group Fighter Command resurrected the airfield as an Emergency Landing Ground (ELG). Like Merston, it was upgraded to a full satellite airfield whereupon it became parented by the sector airfield of Kenley in Surrey. With a good landing area running NE/SW and measuring 5,020 ft, it was used in the Battle of Britain mainly by fighters in trouble, no resident squadrons were based there. Not until May 1941 when the ASR Lysanders of No. 225 Squadron based at Shoreham used it could Friston be called fully operational. Even this was only over the summer months as the field closed every winter whilst further upgrading took place. Several accommodation blocks were built together with a type of watch office and Friston reopened on 15th May 1942.

Although the airfield was originally an ELG which was upgraded to a satellite, 31st May saw it relegated to a K site decoy airfield as dummy Spitfires were erected all over the site. From the air it certainly did give the impression of a busy fighter airfield but obviously not enough, as the Luftwaffe chose to ignore the airfield. As the ruse had not worked, Friston was reinstated to a satellite, and on 14th June 1942 No. 253 (Hyderabad State) Squadron flew their Hurricane IIAs in from Hibaldstow. In the afternoon they were joined by the Hurricane Is of No. 32 Squadron who arrived from West Malling where they had been taking part in Turbinlite operations with 531 Flight (see *Kent Airfields Remembered*).

The two squadrons operated together as a wing carrying out offensive sweeps across the Channel. It had been intended to use the wing during the planned heavy attacks on the Dieppe guns, known as 'Operation Rutter' but these plans were dropped and it was back to offensive duties until 7th July when both squadrons returned to their former airfields. They returned to Friston briefly on 14th August for six days but the period in between saw the first of many attacks to be made upon the airfield.

When both squadrons left Friston, the airfield suddenly became a target for the Luftwaffe. As the Civil Defence records state at the beginning of this chapter, 9th July saw two ME 109s drop two 500 lb bombs on the airfield, returning minutes later to fly across strafing anything in sight with cannon fire. They did this unhindered and as they flew back across the Channel, Friston was left to lick its wounds. One newly erected Blister hangar had been flattened, damage had been caused to the new SHQ and the grass runways had been left badly cratered. All hands were put to work filling in the craters, including the civilian construction gang who were still working on the airfield. Despite their various grumbles they worked well and Friston was back in operation within 16 hours.

Several detachments from the Kenley wing used the airfield during July but it was not until Nos. 32 and 253 Squadrons arrived back at Friston to take part in the Dieppe operation that it became a frontline fighter satellite once more.

The pale tinge of dawn began to break shortly after 3 am on 19th August 1942 as both 32 and 253 pilots stumbled from their beds. The ground crews had been up long before this preparing the aircraft for the great assault. Blinking in the half light, the pilots went to breakfast before 32 Squadron were scrambled at 4.45 am. Twelve Hurricanes rose into the air led by Squadron Leader E Thorn DFM and were soon over the invasion beaches. They were followed by 253 who concentrated on the German gun emplacements around Dieppe. Both squadrons received a fair amount of flak but returned safely to Friston to refuel and rearm before taking off once again for Dieppe. It became obvious to the pilots that all was not going according to plan down below but they were unable to assist the troops apart from endeavouring to keep the area clear of the Luftwaffe and at the same time, cause havoc and destruction among the German guns. By the end of the afternoon many sorties had been flown by the Friston squadrons, who on arriving back at the airfield saw that several badly shot-up aircraft from other units had used the airfield facilities. This was to increase as the war progressed and the rest of 1942 was to see all types dispersed around the field at some time of another. With 'Operation Jubilee' over, 32 left for West Malling on the 20th and 253 departed the same day for Hibaldstow. For the rest of the year, Friston was used occasionally by various detachments but more as an ELG for aircraft in trouble.

Christmas and the New Year saw very little change with detachments coming and going plus the usual selection of 'lame ducks' sitting around. The Luftwaffe however still paid Friston a lot of attention as 21st January indicates when a lone raider dropped a pattern of bombs on the runway, many of them delayed action types. Hastily arrangements were made for an RAF Bomb Disposal team to deal with these but at the same time, someone else had contacted an Army Bomb Disposal team to do likewise. Both teams arrived almost simultaneously and immediately an argument developed over whose responsibility it was to defuse them. Luckily, before it came to blows and pistols at dawn, an amicable arrangement was agreed and both teams shared the bombs.

Another attack by the Luftwaffe on 14th March caused various buildings and a lot of the trees and shrubs surrounding the airfield to catch fire. The station fire service was hard-pressed to contain the building fires on site but luckily the Eastbourne Fire Brigade came to the woodland fires.

It was not until 27th May 1943 that a resident squadron again used Friston, when No. 41 brought their Spitfire XIIs in from Biggin Hill. No. 41 whose motto of 'Seek and destroy' was to prove very appropriate, were mainly employed on countering the many Luftwaffe low level fighter/bomber attacks on coastal targets and airfields within Sussex and Kent. In addition they flew shipping reconnaissance and bomber escort missions.

Their time of success came on 4th June when a dogfight developed off Eastbourne between 41 Squadron and 18 FW 190s. Two were shot down by the squadron whilst another two fell to the AA defences with many of the bombs from the Germans being jettisoned into the sea. 41 remained at Friston until 21st June when they moved over to Westhampnett to be replaced by No. 412 (Falcon) Squadron of the

RCAF. Bringing their Spitfire VBs from Perranporth, they soon settled in and commenced flying Ramrods and Rodeos until 16th July when they left for Redhill in Surrey.

It was the turn of the Polish 306 (Torunski) Squadron to use Friston now as their Spitfire VBs flew over from Gravesend. They were due to join the 2nd TAF in preparation for the invasion of France and stayed at Friston barely a month before departing for Heston on 21st September. With this period of rapid changes, the Belgian 349 Squadron were the next occupants. One of only two Belgian squadrons in Fighter Command, they had originally formed on 10th November 1942 at Ikeja in Nigeria for service in the Belgian Congo. At the end of May 1943 the squadron was transferred to the UK and reformed with Spitfires at Wittering on 5th June 1943, becoming an integral part of 135 wing and flying sweeps over France. They moved down from Acklington to Friston on 22nd October 1943, left on the 26th for Southend but returned to Friston on 10th November for several months. Also based at Friston around this hectic period was the Polish 308 (Krakowski) Squadron who arrived on 7th September with Spitfire IXs. They too were attached to the 2nd TAF and carried out fighter/bomber sweeps before leaving two weeks later.

With the onset of autumn the weather changed and the Belgians had to cope with appalling conditions. The airfield became a bog as the poor ground crews struggled to service the Spitfires either in the open or under leaking, draughty Blister hangars. A very miserable Christmas was spent by the men at Friston and January brought little change. With the airfield now parented by Biggin Hill, the first month of the New Year saw the base used by many more aircraft in distress including many four-engined bombers returning from raids over Germany. The Luftwaffe returned on 22nd January 1944 and dropped several bombs on and around Friston before turning and scurrying back across the Channel. It was with great joy and relief that 349 Belgian Squadron left for Hornchurch on 11th March for they had not really enjoyed their stay. Once again, No. 41 came in flying the Spitfire XII and commenced carrying out Ramrods and Rhubarbs. They had hoped for a greatly improved Friston but found it basically the same as before, bleak and very muddy. Around this time it was rumoured that concrete hardstandings would be built but nothing happened and the ground crews and pilots continued to operate in very difficult conditions. Again, 41 were glad to leave for Bolt Head

The severe winter of 1943/4 was not welcomed by ground crews struggling to service aircraft such as these Spitfire IXs of 349 Squadron (Imperial War Museum).

on 29th April.

With preparations for the invasion of Europe going ahead at a fast pace, the second Belgian Squadron, No. 350, flew into Friston from Peterhead on 25th April. Five days later they were joined by No. 501 (County of Gloucester) Squadron as both units formed a No. 11 Group ADGB wing flying Spitfire VBs. With nearby Tangmere taking over the parenting from Biggin Hill, the wing proceeded to carry out attacks on enemy shipping and enemy airfields in the run-up to D Day.

The Luftwaffe returned to carry out a hit and run raid on Friston on 30th May when several HE 250 kg bombs were dropped just off the runway centre line. This caused the airfield to be out of use for several hours as the task of filling the craters became a priority. By the evening the field was once again operational which was just as well as many American bombers used Friston for emergency landings.

On D Day itself, the wing was airborne early but found very little action. With a first class view of the landings taking place below, 350 and 501's Spitfires found no opposition to their patrols. Similar

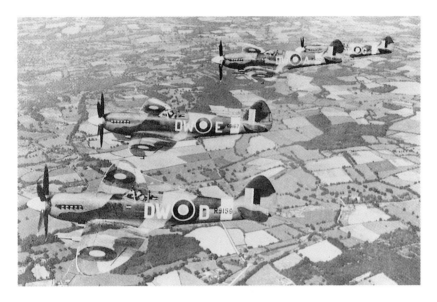

Spitfire XIVs over Friston in 1944. These planes were well-equipped to deal with the scourge of the Doodlebug (Evening Argus).

operations continued for the rest of June until 501 left on 2nd July with the Belgians departing two days later, both squadrons going to Westhampnett.

Once again 41 returned to their old haunt and together with No. 610 (County of Chester) Squadron commenced anti-diver operations. The Doodlebug campaign was now gathering pace and many squadrons were diverted from offensive operations to combat this menace. The XII and XIV marks of Spitfire flown by the squadrons were ideally suited to this type of warfare and the scores of both units began to mount. 41 left to carry on the diver operations from Lympne on the 11th July but 610 remained until 12th September when they too departed to Lympne.

Before that however, a Polish squadron returned to Friston for anti-diver duties on 11th July 1944 when 316 (Warszawski) Squadron brought their Mustang IIIs over from West Malling. The Mustangs were a better platform than the Spitfires for this type of operation, something that was borne out by the fact that 316 had destroyed 50 V1s by the end of July. Day and night the Doodlebugs droned over

Sussex and Kent but many of them never reached their intended target of London. They fell to the guns of the AA defences or the fighters of No. 11 Group. On 27th August, 316 left for Coltishall in Norfolk and were replaced by No. 131 (County of Kent) Squadron flying Spitfire VIIs. They carried out several anti-diver operations but with the Allies bombing many of the launch sites, the V1 campaign began to peter out and 131 were switched to bomber escort patrols.

Friston was still accepting many 'lame ducks' and nightly the locals were kept awake by heavy bombers circling the airfield awaiting their turn to land. 131 was the last full fighter squadron to be based at Friston as the rundown to victory began. They became non-operational in November and prepared to move to India. Apart from the diversions that landed daily and nightly, Friston was no longer of use as a fighter satellite. It returned to its origins as an ELG and saw a resurgence of use early in 1945 when No. 7 Fighter Command Servicing Unit took up residence. The 18th April saw the Auster Vs of 666 (RCAF) Squadron arrive from Andover but they stayed for just

Hardly 'a piece of cake'! A grimly realistic airfield fire filmed for the TV series of that name in 1988 (Evening Argus).

a month before moving across the Channel. By 25th May 1945 Friston had been reduced to care and maintenance. The end of the war was in sight and the battle area had moved to central Europe.

Dunsfold took over responsibility for Friston in June, this being transferred back to Tangmere in February 1946 before the site was finally derequisitioned on the 8th April 1946 and the land was returned to the Church Commissioners.

One summer's day during 1988, 44 years after the last Spitfire had left, two Spitfires roared along the Sussex coastline, pulled up over Seven Sisters cliffs, circled the airfield and coming in low over the hedgerows settled down on the grass. Were they in distress? Not really, for they had arrived to film part of the TV series 'Piece of Cake'. Cardboard and plastic replica Spitfires sprang up all over the airfield, props to ensure that the film looked authentic. For several weeks Friston once again was alive with activity until, with the filming finished, the Spitfires left the airfield and silence settled. Finally Friston was laid to rest.

Very few signs remain today of the RAF occupation, though the intrepid historian walking across the site can certainly feel a sense of history. Maybe there is still a ghost waiting to be freed. Who knows!

8

MERSTON

Even before the Second World War had started, plans had been drawn up for the establishment of dummy airfields, or decoy sites as they eventually came to be known. Their obvious aim was to entice the Luftwaffe to drop their bombs on these sites and thus save the main airfields from destruction. From 1940 onwards most main RAF airfields had decoys, all of them falling into the following categories:

K sites: RAF day decoys simulating satellite airfields and usually equipped with dummy aircraft and buildings

Q sites: RAF night decoys complete with Drem airfield lighting (Drem lighting comprised the actual runway lighting, the approach lighting and the outer circle lighting. Mainly designed for bomber airfields, 20 fighter stations received it as well as several decoy sites)

QF sites: Small fields lit with fire to represent buildings or blazing oil installations, ie fuel dumps

QL sites: Fields with decoy lighting representing anything other than airfields

In Sussex, some of these decoys were to be built at Alciston, Cuckmere Haven, Frant and Camber Castle but of equal importance to the RAF was the establishment of satellite airfields, one of which was built at Merston, just 1½ miles from Chichester. Merston spent the whole of its existence as a satellite to Tangmere and never really came into its own. This is not to say that it was of any less importance for it was in constant use throughout the conflict, but it never really received the praise of which it was worthy.

Surveys of the site were carried out in early 1939 and with the land duly requisitioned in July, Merston was planned to become a K site decoy and not really a proper satellite airfield. With the immediate build-up during 1940 of nearby Tangmere, Merston was upgraded to become a full satellite airfield with domestic buildings and hangarage. Work began immediately on levelling and drainage, all this continuing whilst the Battle of Britain raged overhead. With the bad weather hampering work over the autumn and winter of 1940, the airfield was not ready until spring 1941. It opened with a full complement of administration and technical buildings plus six Blister hangars and some fighter protection pens.

It fell to No. 145 Squadron, part of the Tangmere wing, to inaugurate the new station when they flew their Spitfire IIBs over from Tangmere on 28th May 1941. The squadron had been very successful during the Battle of Britain and now their IIBs were employed on Rhubarbs, low level strike operations against targets in occupied Europe. The IIB mark of Spitfire was ideal in this rôle with its four 0.303 guns plus two 20mm cannons proving a devastating punch, but they carried out very few operations from Merston before flying up to Catterick on 28th July 1941.

The same day No. 41 Squadron arrived from Catterick to replace them. Equipped with the Spitfire I and IIA, they converted to the VB immediately and commenced Rhubarbs. Enjoying a fair amount of success, they spent the rest of the summer and autumn at Merston, leaving shortly before Christmas for the other Tangmere satellite of Westhampnett. The winter rains turned the airfield into a field of mud and for three months it became unserviceable. The construction gangs arrived in the spring of 1942 but did very little to ensure the airfield did not suffer in the future. It was mainly left to dry out naturally and by 1st April had done so as No. 41 returned. They were joined in May by No. 131 (County of Kent) Squadron who brought their VBs down from Llanbedr. Bomber escort duties were now carried out by both squadrons in addition to the usual Rhubarbs. 131 was unusual in that it was one of the few units to be funded from donations given by the people of Kent. In return, each aircraft had the name of a Kentish town written on the fuselage and all the aircraft carried the Kent Invicta. The squadron motto was also 'Invicta' meaning 'Unconquered', and this association with the county was carried on throughout the life of the squadron.

Both squadrons operated from Merston as part of the Tangmere wing and with No. 412 (Falcon) Squadron of the RCAF relieving No. 41 in June, there began a period of intense escort work as the run-up to 'Operation Jubilee' began. On 19th August, the day of the Dieppe landings, 412 moved back to Tangmere leaving 131 to operate alone from the satellite. They were scrambled early in the morning to intercept what was thought to be a force of enemy aircraft approaching the Kent coast but which turned out to be an American aircraft being harassed by the Luftwaffe. Unfortunately the American Boston was shot down and 131 escorted the ASR Walrus sent to pick up the crew. By 8.50 am they were over the beach-heads but so were the FW 190s. Several dogfights began as the enemy desperately tried to stop the landings from taking place. 131 fared well, shooting down one FW 190 for no loss to themselves. They returned to Merston to refuel and rearm and were escorting a force of bombers back to the beaches by midday. With this uneventful sortie over, it was back to base once again. Thirty minutes later they were airborne again and heading for Dieppe. This time the Luftwaffe were waiting but 131 managed to shoot down two Dornier 217s and damage another for no loss. Jubilant with their success, they returned once again to Merston and were airborne again at 5.30 pm for the last sortie of the day. As they flew over the army below attempting to gain a foothold at Dieppe, they witnessed the slaughter of many of the men. The squadron also had their problems as they went into attack a force of JU 88s attempting to bomb the Allies. They shot down one and damaged two others before some of their own Spitfires were damaged. One of their aircraft was severely damaged, but managed to reach Selsey before ditching in the sea, the pilot being rescued with just slight injuries. The remaining aircraft though full of holes, made Merston safely. At dusk, 131 were stood down and although their own success was cause for celebration, the failure of 'Operation Jubilee' was not.

On the 22nd both 131 and 412 moved over to Tangmere and Merston was taken over by the Americans. The Spitfire VBs of the 307th fighter squadron of the 31st Fighter Group, 8th Air Force, looked strangely out of place with their American markings but they did sterling work on bomber escort work. They were later transferred to operations in connection with 'Operation Torch', the invasion of French North Africa in October 1942. With their departure, Merston was left to the construction gangs who attempted to stop once and

In August 1942 Merston temporarily hosted 307 Fighter Squadron of 31st Fighter Group, 8th Air Force, who flew their Spitfire VBs on bomber escort duties (Imperial War Museum).

for all the waterlogging that took place every winter. Two Sommerfeld Track runways were laid, the main SW/NE runway extending to 4,776 ft.

Merston reopened in May 1943 with increased accommodation allowing a strength of 80 officers and 1,200 other ranks to be based there. It fell to a RNZAF squadron, No. 485 to bring Merston back to a front-line satellite station when they flew their Spitfire VBs over from Westhampnett on 21st May 1943 to continue bomber escort sorties. Joined by the Hurricanes of 184 Squadron from Eastchurch on the 31st, Merston was up to full strength for a short period. The Hurricanes were the Mk. IV fighter/bombers and were at the airfield purely to allow the pilots the maxium period of time practising rocket firing on the nearby ranges. When they left on 12th June, the Typhoons of No. 174 (Mauritius) Squadron arrived from Gravesend for similar practice. By 1st July both 485 and 174 had left and Merston stayed empty and desolate for a month.

It was the turn of a Canadian unit to use the base next as Nos. 402 (Winnipeg Bear) and 416 (City of Oshawa), both part of the Canadian Digby Wing, arrived on 7th and 9th August respectively. They were

143

A Typhoon IB of the type flown by 181 Squadron, who moved to Merston at the end of 1943 (Air Britain).

attached to No. 11 Group, Fighter Command for Roadsted operations and when No. 118 Squadron brought their Spitfires over from Westhampnett, Merston became decidedly overcrowded. The three squadrons carried out many fighter sweeps against enemy shipping with considerable success and very little loss.

By late 1943, plans were well advanced for the invasion of Europe and Merston had been earmarked for future use by the Tactical Air Force. In preparation the Canadian wing moved out and a Typhoon wing comprising Nos. 181, 182 and 247 (China British) Squadrons arrived from New Romney, one of the ALGs in Kent. The wing was renamed No. 124 Airfield on 15th November 1943 and began a series of devastating attacks on a variety of targets in Northern France. Increasingly the attacks were against Noball sites, the V1 launching pads in both Holland and France. It had been known for some time that Hitler had been planning a revenge weapon in the form of some kind of pilotless robot with rocket propulsion and it was further known that the strange ramplike structures seen in woods and quarries were the means of launching them. This type of operation continued over the Christmas period and although the wing left Merston for brief periods at Eastchurch and Odiham, they were back at the airfield to continue the Noball site attacks until April when it became the turn of the Free French to use Merston.

As No. 124 Airfield departed to Hurn, they were replaced by No. 145 Airfield from Perranporth. Nos. 329 (GC 1/2 'Cigones'), 340 (GC IV/2 'Ile de France') and 341 (GC 111/2 'Alsace') Squadrons arrived on 17th April 1944. Equipped with Spitfire IXBs, they began extensive sweeps across France in preparation for 'Operation Overlord', the Allied invasion of Europe. The wing suffered a blow shortly after commencing these attacks when two of the aircraft collided killing both pilots. Conversion to dive-bombing attacks began in May and on D Day itself, 6th June, the wing provided low level cover for the troop-carrying ships. Similar operations continued for the next week giving the wing some success when they became entangled with a formation of JU 88s, managing to shoot one down for no loss.

By 22nd June the wing had moved over to the ALG at Funtington as Nos. 80, 229 and 274 Squadrons with Spitfire IXs moved in briefly from Detling. When they left on 27th June, the last unit to use

Two doubtlessly chilled Merston ground crew watch while a third prepares a Spitfire IX of 349 Squadron for take-off (Imperial War Museum).

Merston arrived, once again for a very brief period. This unit was a very mixed bag indeed comprising Nos. 30, 303 (Kosciusko) manned by Polish personnel, and 402 (Winnipeg Bear), the Canadian squadron that had served at Merston before. Together they made up 142 Wing with Spitfires whose job it was to escort the bombers now taking the war back to Germany. By 27th June they had gone and Merston was silent. This time it was final as the Allies pushed towards Germany and the need for satellite airfields in the south of the country receded. By 21st August, ATC facilities had been withdrawn as the airfield was reduced to care and maintenance. The Sommerfeld Tracking was removed and permission was given to the local farmer to use the field for limited grazing.

The last use made of Merston was on 16th March 1945 when the domestic accommodation was used by 700 men attached to the Air Disarmament Units. They left in May and the buildings were leased to the Admiralty for storage purposes until the end of the year.

For a satellite airfield, Merston had a very active career. Despite its early waterlogging problems, it is able to take its place with pride among the other satellite airfields. There is little left however to remind us of its career except pieces of the concrete perimeter track and a few domestic buildings still left standing.

9
THE ADVANCED
LANDING GROUNDS

On 4th May 1942, the following memo was sent to all departments of the Air Ministry by a senior staff officer: 'One of the limiting factors of the intensive operations envisaged in the Pas-de-Calais area is the number of landing grounds available in Kent and Sussex. Therefore, at least six more airfields should if possible be provided in this area. The construction of permanent airfields would prove too long a process. They would not require full facilities normally provided at permanent stations but it would, however, be necessary to provide runways. All major repair work on aircraft would be carried out on permanent stations.'

It was already felt by many during these early stages of the war that there would be a need for more temporary landing strips once plans for an invasion on the continent were finalised. Already the Air Ministry planning staff were working on a proposed landing strip in the Pas-de-Calais region which was codenamed 'Operation Hadrian', but the Dieppe disaster in August 1942 ensured the operation never went ahead. In fact all future plans for an immediate landing in France were cancelled and all efforts fell upon the construction of ALGs in the south east which would be needed when the Allied assault on Europe did take place.

It was proposed to use a standard specification of two metal runways, one 1,600 yds long and the other 1,400 yds long with a width of 50 yards and a perimeter track as close to the runways as possible. Two Blister hangars would be erected initially with a further two as and when demand and building labour was available. Accommodation was to be in tents supplemented by the acquisition of local large houses. The number of aircraft using each strip was submitted to be 50 with explosive materials such as fuel and ammunition stored in woodland areas some way from the ALG in case of enemy attacks. The sites chosen were mainly poor quality farmland but it was not always possible to do this and in cases where farmers were reluctant to give up their fields and grazing land, there was compulsory requisition, something that upset many farmers especially in the case of Apuldram and Selsey in Sussex. With civilian labour employed on building the larger airfields, it was left to military construction gangs to build the airstrips. This was to prove invaluable in 1944 when the Allies had established a hold in Europe and landing strips on the continent were needed quickly.

Like its neighbouring county of Kent, Sussex had many ALGs within its border. The original plan allowed for 15 possible sites in the Biggin Hill, Hornchurch, Kenley and Tangmere sectors but as the war progressed, the plans became even more ambitious. By mid 1942, the areas under consideration had extended to Weston-Super-Mare and beyond and it was planned that they would all be ready for use by spring 1943. Seventy two possible sites were under consideration but this was whittled down to a short list of 25. Exclusion of two more brought the final number to 23, which were planned to be built all in the south east and along the south coast. Thus they would all be constructed along the land mass nearest to the point of the proposed Allied landings in France.

Both the RAF and the Army were instrumental in the planning of the construction units that would build the ALGs, and with most of them planned to be in operation by mid 1943, work began straight away on clearing and grading the sites. In Sussex, Apuldram and Selsey were constructed solely by the RAF gangs whereas Deanland, built later than the others, was constructed by the Airfield Construction Group of the Royal Engineers. However, weather and manpower problems arose and this delayed completion of most of the sites until the end of June 1943.

With most of the ALGs just open fields, the problem of a serviceable surface for aircraft to use was solved with the laying of Sommerfeld Track across the proposed runways. A heavy steel netting pinned to the ground, it suffered problems if aircraft landed heavily, this resulting in the ripping up of large areas of the track. The second type was named Square Mesh Track and was a development of the welded mesh used in roads and other structures. This type of surface generally succeeded the Sommerfeld Track during spring 1944. Some of the ALGs however were used solely by the Americans and they had designed their own surface tracking known as Pierced Steel Plank. This was produced in such large quantities that when it became surplus to American requirements several grass airfields in Britain were also using it.

After the Allies had landed in France in June 1944 and were beginning the big push towards Berlin, most of the ALGs were abandoned as the squadrons flew to similar sites in Europe. They had served their purpose admirably and a large part of the aviation history of Sussex took place at them. The major Sussex ALGs were as follows.

Apuldram

As with many of the proposed sites for ALGs, Apuldram had its fair share of objectors, the main one being the Ministry of Agriculture. It was originally an expanse of fertile grassland which was considered good soil for growing crops and thus adding to the war effort generally, and the Ministry fought hard to retain it. A survey during 1942 for possible ALG sites had earmarked Apuldram as particularly suitable and a formal requisition for the land was granted to the Air Ministry in December 1942. As previously mentioned, the RAF personnel of the construction gangs moved in during February 1943, and levelling and removal of obstructions began immediately. Right up to this point, the Ministry of Agriculture had objected and in order to pacify them, the Air Ministry agreed that if after construction Apuldram was not in immediate use, grazing permission would be given. That issue settled, the RAF gangs began to lay Sommerfeld Track on the proposed runways, in this case in the shape of a crucifix. Despite difficult weather, the ALG was ready by the end of May. It came into immediate use thus denying the Ministry of Agriculture a chance to graze cattle or sheep. After the setting up of primitive tented accommodation for the personnel, No. 124 Airfield of the 2nd Tactical Air Force arrived with the Typhoon fighter/bomber. Comprising Nos. 175, 181 and 182 Squadrons, it flew in from Lasham on 2nd June 1943, and by nightfall the aircraft were dispersed among the trees surrounding the airfield.

The Typhoon had got off to a bad start when it initially entered with the RAF. Intended as an interceptor fighter, it failed miserably but found its true rôle as a fighter/bomber and close support aircraft. 124 Airfield used the aircraft with devastating effect for as far back as December 1942, 175 and 181 Squadrons had operated the Typhoon with two 250 lb bombs slung beneath each wing. They had used them against enemy shipping in the 'Channel Stop' campaign with deadly accuracy and this continued with attacks on ground targets during their period at Apuldram.

What did not please the personnel of 124 Airfield was the tented accommodation and the very meagre field kitchens. The surface of Apuldram also left a lot to be desired for it could be very moist and swampy. After the comparative luxury of Lasham, the men wondered just what they had done to deserve this seeming injustice.

After expecting comfortable accommodation at Tangmere, the Czech personnel of 312 Squadron were not impressed with the primitive living conditions of Apuldram (M. A. Liskutin).

150

124 Airfield began operations on 4th June against enemy airfields and there followed a series of similar attacks against communication centres and radar sites. The Typhoons suffered very few problems and no losses during their stay, which ended on 1st July as the airfield moved to the Kent ALGs, 175 Squadron going to Lydd and 181 and 182 moving to New Romney a day later. With their departure, silence descended on Apuldram. The site was left with a care and maintenance party in situ for almost ten months. During this period, the Air Ministry kept their word and it was used for occasional grazing. This gave the site the appearance of being just a farmer's meadow and thus attracted no attention from enemy aircraft. It came back into use on 4th April 1944 when 134 Airfield flying Spitfire IXs arrived. This was a unit consisting entirely of Czechoslovak personnel. 310 Squadron flew in from Southend on 3rd April 1944 where they had been on a dive-bombing and ground attack course. 312 and 313 arrived a day later from Mendlesham, all three squadrons being classed as a ground attack unit within the Army Support Command.

It came as a surprise to the Czechs to be posted to Apuldram for they had been convinced that Tangmere was to be their next posting. Nice warm Tangmere with its brick and wooden accommodation, nice warm mess with well cooked food. Who on earth would want to be posted to a less than comfortable ALG? To crown it all, wintry weather was still persisting in March 1944 as the night temperature sometimes fell below freezing. However, Tangmere was only a short distance away and frequent trips there made life a little more bearable.

In order to ease the problem of aircraft sitting at dispersal and slowly sinking into the wet surface, metal hardstandings were provided for the Spitfires. Not to be outdone in the matter of comfort, the Czechs requisitioned several farm cottages nearby and took it in turns to sleep in a manner of warmth and dryness. Life at Apuldram suddenly became not so bad after all.

For the Czech squadrons, Apuldram was to provide a variety of targets with dive-bombing attacks against V1 and V2 installations, bomber escorts and offensive patrols. Railways and marshalling yards seemed to be attractive targets for them and in one outstanding operation one of the pilots, F/O Franta Miejnecky, delivered a 500 lb bomb straight into the entrance of Rouen tunnel bringing down the

Czech pilots of 312 Squadron pose in front of a Spitfire IXB. Among other duties the squadron attacked V1 and V2 launching sites (M. A. Liskutin).

surrounding hillside and thus closing the railway for the rest of the war.

For 134 Airfield, D Day began at first light and the Czechs reverted to their original fighter rôle for this operation. They patrolled over the beaches and due to the lack of enemy opposition, maintained air superiority throughout that first day. On D Day plus two, 312 Squadron shot down two Focke Wulf 190s, both of them going to the guns of F/O Ota Smik. The following days saw the entire airfield remaining in action over the landing area and although several Spitfires were lost, it had been a successful time for the Czech squadrons.

They moved to Tangmere on 22nd June 1944 and went straight into 'Diver' operations. Six days later it was the turn of the Poles to use Apuldram when No. 131 Wing flew their Spitfire IXs the short hop from the ALG at Chailey. Nos. 302 (Poznan), 308 (Krakow) and 317 (Wilno) settled in and began offensive operations over Europe. They flew ahead of the advancing army dive-bombing enemy positions and attacking moving columns of troops before they too departed on 16th July to Ford and thence to France.

With the Allies pushing into Europe, France was indeed where the majority of the 2nd TAF went, and after the departure of 131 Wing no further use was made of Apuldram. By November 1944 it had been derequisitioned and 5027 Works Squadron had moved in by January 1945 to remove the Sommerfeld Track. The entire site was returned to the Ministry of Agriculture and today not one visible sign of its existence remains.

Bognor

It was on 9th August 1932 that the National Aviation Day display first took place at Bognor. It came back on 27th August a year later, again on 17th August 1934 and finally on 9th August 1935. By this time, negotiations were taking place between Alan Cobham and the local council to build a municipal airport, but by 1935 nothing had materialised and the idea was abandoned. It lay virtually forgotten until the surveys for prospective ALG sites carried out during 1942 noted that Bognor had been a candidate for an airport. It was not the original site however that eventually became the ALG.

Once again, there were objections from the Ministry of Agriculture but these were overruled and approval was given for the clearance and grading to begin by December 1942. The weather proved kind and work progressed swiftly culminating in the laying of SW/NE and NW/SE runways strengthened with Sommerfeld Track. Again, tented accommodation was to be provided with field kitchen facilities but with no hangarage for aircraft. Officially declared open on 1st July 1943, Bognor was to be parented by Tangmere and like most of the ALGs, was intended for use by the 2nd TAF.

It saw immediate use as No. 122 Airfield flew in with Spitfire VBs on 1st June, shortly after the handover. No. 122 (Bombay) Squadron from Eastchurch and No. 602 (City of Glasgow) from Fairlop arrived and were joined on the 6th by No. 19 Squadron from Gravesend flying the VC mark of Spitfire. They used the local practice ranges to perfect ground-attack operations and carried out several 'Ramrods' over the continent. It was a brief stay and by 1st July, they had departed to the Kent ALGs of Kingsnorth and Newchurch (see *Kent Airfields Remembered*).

Upgrading of the site took place when hardstanding was provided for future use and several Blister hangars constructed. With the expected invasion of Europe during 1944, Bognor like most of the ALGs was to see a very hectic period. It began when No. 132 Airfield of No. 84 Group, 2nd TAF arrived from North Weald on 31st March 1944. The unit comprised No. 66 and Nos. 331 and 332 Squadrons, the latter two with all Norwegian aircrew personnel. They flew the IX fighter/bomber mark of Spitfire which was a stop-gap version prior to the VIII which was to be fitted with the new Merlin 61 engine. The IX however proved to be a very good version and together with the Mk.V, became the most widely used mark.

132 Airfield carried out the usual offensive sorties, 332 Squadron achieving considerable success on 11th April when they destroyed six enemy aircraft on the ground whilst flying a 'Ranger' operation. As the preparations for D Day began, the operations increased with attacks on coastal enemy positions interspersed with V1 site attacks. The 6th June saw the Norwegians flying beach-head patrols and further attacks on rocket sites. Flying over the advancing Allied forces, their hearts were gladdened for they knew that upon the success of this invasion, victory would not be far away, and with it their own liberation. Very little contact was made with the enemy but the patrols continued until 21st June when the Wing moved over to Tangmere.

Bognor was immediately occupied by No. 83 Group Support Unit who came in from Redhill, fearful that the V1 crashes in the vicinity of Redhill would cause the loss of many reserve aircraft if they landed on the airfield itself. Spitfires, Typhoons and Mustangs were dispersed around the field and hastily camouflaged in case a German snooper unexpectedly arrived. With so many aircraft movements Bognor saw some serious incidents, but considering the amount of aircraft constantly flying in and out the number was very minimal.

By 25th September 1944 they had gone and silence descended upon Bognor. With the front line now over the Channel, the ALG was no longer required and the site was released by November. The steel matting was removed and by 1945 the ALG had been returned to the landowners.

This was not the end, for Bognor resurfaced during the 1980s but not on the original site of the ALG. It had moved across the county a little and until 1994 was once again a thriving airfield. Now closed, the layout remains a fine example of how many of the ALGs in Sussex must have looked during 1943/44.

Chailey

As mentioned in the introductory paragraphs, of the 72 sites originally selected, 23 were eventually chosen. A letter was sent from the Air Ministry to all interested parties including of course the county and local councils and local landowners, concerning the choice of sites. Of particular interest was the letter sent from the Air Ministry on 15th September 1942 to Sussex County Council stating that at a meeting held at the Ministry it was agreed that the following sites originally under consideration had been abandoned – Shortgate, Hurstpierpoint, Henfield, Ripe and Halland. Not abandoned however although situated in thick Sussex woodland was Chailey, surveyed during the 1942 appraisal. The plans were sent to Fighter Command and approval was given by December. Levelling and grading took place from January 1943, with two Sommerfeld Track runways and taxiways being built and ready by summer 1943. As it was not used immediately the field was offered to the Ministry of Agriculture who used it for grazing during the rest of 1943 and through to spring 1944. In anticipation of its use for D Day and after four Blister hangars and hardcore standings were built, in April 1944, No. 131 Airfield, 84 Group of the 2nd TAF arrived from the nearby ALG at Deanland.

131 was formed from Polish personnel who had escaped from France after the German invasion and comprised 302 (Poznan), 308 (Krakow) and 312 (Wilenski) Squadrons. They flew Spitfire IXs in the fighter/bomber rôle and were soon engaged on 'Ranger' operations over France. Occasional heavy landings caused much of the steel tracking to rip up causing damage to aircraft tyres and undercarriage alike but Chailey persisted with Sommerfeld Tracking and due to its short operational life was never fitted with PSP.

Renamed 131 Wing on 15th May 1944, the Poles prepared for D Day as invasion stripes were painted on the Spitfires to make them more recognisable. Briefings were carried out under strict security, and the task nominated to 131 Wing was low level cover over the invading Allies. This they carried out with great enthusiasm over D Day itself and on until 28th June when they left for the ALG at Apuldram.

Chailey was used solely by 131 Wing and when they departed, no further use was made of the site. Compared with the other ALGs, it had a very short career and the landowners were pressing for the derequisition of Chailey by October 1944. It eventually came on 20th January 1945 when a Works Flight arrived to remove the Sommerfeld Tracking. One may well ask why with so many other ALGs in the county it was really necessary to construct Chailey and use it for barely two months. In contrast to the abandoned sites mentioned in the opening paragraph, obviously it was thought that this one offered more prospects than the laymen could see. Chailey was fully returned to its natural state and today just an Air Ministry plan of the ALG in the hands of the local farmer reminds us of its existence.

Coolham

Many of the squadrons sent to ALGs went for one main purpose, that of gaining experience of operating from airfields with spartan facilities. This was something that they could expect on their arrival on the continent and the experience gained on the ALGs in SE England certainly prepared them for the worst of operational conditions. To the personnel, the worst part was the primitive living conditions applicable to all the sites including Coolham near Horsham. However, the tents in this case were supplemented by farmhouses nearby and the village of Coolham itself was to be very receptive to the Polish squadrons that used the ALG.

Once again, approved in 1942, built during 1943 and in use by April 1944, it had a short but hectic career. Two Sommerfeld Tracking runways were laid, the main SE/NW being 4,500 ft long, and like Chailey the site was released for grazing until 1st April 1944 when No. 133 Airfield flew in from Heston. Initially a Polish unit with Nos. 306 (Torun) and 315 (Deblin) Squadrons, they were joined by No. 129

Polish airmen of 306 Squadron at Coolham, June 1944. 133 Wing of the TAF, to which the squadron belonged, played an important part in the run-up to D Day (Polish Institute).

(Mysore) Squadron from Llanbedr on the 3rd of the month. Both 315 and 129 had recently converted to the Mustang III but 306 brought their Spitfire VBs to Coolham, converting to the Mustang three days later. The Merlin engined variant of this aircraft proved a great success with the units and with the first operational sorties being carried out on 26th April 1944, the rest of the month and early May saw the airfield carrying out Ramrods and Rangers with a fair degree of success.

Renamed No. 133 Wing of the TAF on 15th May, the Poles began the run-up to D Day with deep penetration operations far into Europe. On the day itself the Wing were not called upon for the initial sorties but by mid-day they had been scrambled to escort a unit of aircraft tugs with gliders. This operation went well, with 129 Squadron shooting down an FW 190, one of the few German fighters to be seen that day. As the Poles flew back from the escort mission they looked down upon wave after wave of Allied soldiers advancing into Europe. With very little enemy activity in the air, the Allies certainly had complete command over the assault area.

There was very little rest after D Day as the Mustangs continued low level reconnaissance and further Ramrod operations. These finally ended on 22nd June when the Wing transferred to Holmsley South, being replaced at Coolham by No. 135 Wing eight days later. The Spitfire IXs of Nos. 222 (Natal), 349 (Belgian) and 485 Squadrons flew the short hop from Selsey and began fighter/bomber operations from the ALG. For four days they harrassed the German troops trying to stop the Allies advance and the enemy suffered badly from the Spitfire operations. By 4th July they had moved over to Funtington ALG and Coolham was left deserted. Clearance had begun by October with the Sommerfeld Tracking finally being lifted by the New Year of 1945. The ALG was not entirely cleared, for today traces of the hardcore perimeter track are still to be seen, but the site itself has returned to agriculture.

Deanland

Although Ripe was the site of a prospective ALG, the Air Ministry decided to abandon it. However, an ALG was built at Deanland, no great distance from Ripe and today this remains a very pleasant and very active little airfield. It was originally surveyed during 1942 and initial preparation of the ground began in the autumn of that year. On 2nd July 1943, No. 16 Airfield Construction Group of the Royal Engineers arrived to lay two Sommerfeld Track runways at 90° to each other, one being 1,600 yds and the other 1,400 yds long. They were flanked by parallel taxiways with four small concrete hardstandings. Four Blister hangars were hastily erected but once again, no brick accommodation. It was parented by RAF Friston but came into use long before it was intended when two aircraft made emergency landings there. It officially opened on 1st April 1944 when No. 131 Airfield arrived with Spitfire IXs. A Polish unit comprising Nos. 302 (Poznan), 308 (Krakow) and 317 (Wilno), they carried out intensive training in the fighter/bomber rôle with the occasional operational sortie into Europe looking for targets of opportunity. With 302 moving to Southend on 12th April and returning to Deanland on the 14th, the unit moved to the ALG at Chailey on 26th April.

The ALG remained empty for three days, then 149 Airfield came to Deanland. No. 64 Squadron with Spitfire VCs flew in from Coltishall in Norfolk, 611 (West Lancs) also from Coltishall, arrived with Spitfire VBs, and 234 (Madras Presidency) with Spitfire VIs from Bolt Head. Although a very mixed bag of Spitfires, they carried out escort duties to a variety of light bombers intended to soften up the enemy.

No. 611 laid claim to being the first Allied squadron airborne on D Day when they were called at 3 am to provide air cover over the British landings at Gold and the American landings at Omaha beaches. They saw the initial stages of 'Overlord' and with very little German opposition, were able to see the success below and report it when they landed back at Deanland. The rest of the Wing escorted tugs and gliders to the drop zone and after the initial stages of 'Overlord' the Wing carried out offensive operations over Europe.

Being one of the larger ALGs, Deanland was always a tempting site to land when seen by returning bombers in trouble. Very often badly damaged B.17s would see the ALG and crashland onto the Sommerfeld Tracking, ripping it up in the process. Sometimes as many as six aircraft would be seen around the strip, many of them not being able to fly again. In these cases, the aircraft were taken away piece by piece by the USAAF to their resident bases, usually in East Anglia. Needless to say, these incidents played havoc with the day to day operations of Deanland.

With the V1 activity over SE England beginning on 12 June 1944, the ALG lay very close to the combat zone. After 149 Airfield left for Harrowbeer in late June, Deanland became an anti-diver airfield when Nos 91 (Nigeria) and 322 (Dutch) Squadrons arrived from the main anti-diver airfield of West Malling in Kent (see *Kent Airfields Remembered*). Both squadrons had achieved good results in shooting down the doodlebugs whilst at Malling with 91 having a credit of 184, and 322 with a credit of 108. This success continued at Deanland as No. 345 (Free French) Squadron flew in on 16th August 1944 with Spitfire VBs to join the two other anti-diver squadrons. By this time, however, the pace of V1 launchings from sites in France and Holland had lessened due to the swift progress of the Allied invasion, and the diver operations became fewer and fewer. When the V1 launch operations finally ended in France on 1st September, some units did move to Holland but as far as ground launched missiles went, the offensive was over.

The three squadrons prepared to leave Deanland but it was not until October that 91 finally went to Biggin Hill followed by Nos. 322 and 345 who went to Fairwood Common. Deanland's use was over and a works flight moved in quickly to remove the tracking and the site was finally released in January 1945. Deanland lay dormant for a number of years and it slowly returned to agriculture. In recent years Deanland has been resurrected and is now a thriving airfield, popular with small aircraft owners.

Funtington

With the constant friction between the Air Ministry and the Ministry of Agriculture regarding the siting of the ALGs, in its wisdom the former did try to choose poor quality farmland. This, plus the usage of ready built ALGs being released for grazing until required, did appease the agricultural lobby somewhat. Other sites, however, were just not up for discussion or compromise and into this category fell Funtington. Originally selected purely as a landing ground for aircraft in distress or as an overflow or satellite to a neighbouring airfield, Funtington was looked at during 1942. Approval was given for a landing ground; it was upgraded to an ALG in February 1943 and the laying of two Sommerfeld Track runways enabled the newly formed No. 130 Airfield to move from Odiham on 15th September. Nos 4 and 268 Squadrons flew their Mustang Is to Funtington from the comforts of Odiham to begin reconnaissance patrols along the French coast. Not as powerful as the Mustang III, the Mk. I was fine at lower altitudes but handicapped by the lack of power at higher altitudes. Many squadrons, including the two at Funtington, were attached to Army Co-operation Command of the 2nd TAF and in this capacity, the Mustang I supplemented the Tomahawk squadrons. Shortly after their arrival at the ALG, bad weather set in for a period but 130 Airfield were to use their aircraft to good advantage once the bad spell lifted.

Reconnaissance and Ranger patrols were the order of the day until 130 Airfield returned to Odiham on 6th October 1943. The ALG was upgraded to include concrete and hardcore taxiways and hardstandings together with four Blister hangars. Formally handed over on 1st April 1944 to the TAF, No. 143 Airfield arrived with Nos. 438 (Wild Cat), 439 (Westmount) and 440 (City of Ottawa and Beaver) Squadrons bringing their Typhoon IBs over from Hurn. They flew fighter/bomber operations against Noball sites in Northern France, their aircraft being very effective in this rôle. Commanded by Wing Commander R T P Davidson, the Canadians dive-bombed every suspect V1 site, part of the Allied 'Crossbow' bombing offensive which had started in December 1943 against all the missile sites, for it was hoped that the continual bombardment would finally put paid to any projected terror offensive against the British mainland. As history records, it did not but the continual attacks on all known and suspect Noball sites continued.

The Typhoons returned to Hurn on 20th April and were replaced by No. 144 Airfield, once again an all Canadian unit. 441 (Silver Fox), 442 (Caribou) and 443 (Hornet) Squadrons flew in with Spitfire IXBs to begin escort operations. The Wing was commanded by the legendary Wing Commander J E 'Johnnie' Johnson who was eventually to become the highest scoring Allied fighter pilot, with a final total of 38 accredited victories. Day after day the Wing roamed over Europe with great success. One particular day had mixed fortunes; good in that the Wing shot down six FW 190s, but not so good in that they lost two aircraft, one crashlanding with the pilot becoming a POW and another killed when he was shot down. There were constant operations of all types carried out from Funtington by the Wing with each sortie bringing them into contact with many FW 190s. The Canadians transferred to Ford just before D Day but the ALG was soon to see an even more intense period.

Funtington came under the umbrella of 122 Wing, No. 83 Group of the TAF when, on 14th May 1944, 65 and 122 Squadrons arrived with Mustang IIIs. As soon as they had arrived, some of the pilots were ushered into a hush-hush briefing concerning a new type of Ranger operation. Three days later, five Mustangs from 65 Squadron and two from 122 crossed the North Sea to Aalborg in Denmark and achieved total surprise over the enemy held airfields. The surprise was amplified by the success the seven aircraft achieved. Five Junkers 88s, one Heinkel 177, one Messerschmitt 109, two Junkers W34s and two Arado 196s fell to the bombs and cannons of the Mustangs. Two pilots were shot down, one making it back to England via the

Resistance movement, but the entire Ranger was hailed as a great success.

No. 19 Squadron also equipped with Mustangs joined 122 Wing in time for D Day when all three squadrons escorted Coastal Command Beaufighters on anti U-boat patrols and later in the day escorted troop carriers and glider formations over the beaches. After D Day the Wing achieved a fair degree of success when three FW 190s and five ME 109s fell to the Mustangs for the loss of two of ours. Similar intensive operations continued with the Luftwaffe staging just a few appearances until the 15th June when the Wing moved over to Ford in preparation for flying to forward continental air strips.

It was now the turn of 123 Wing, with Nos. 198 and 609 (West Riding) Squadrons, to bring their Typhoons to Funtington. Arriving in the morning, they were joined in the afternoon by Nos. 164 (Argentine-British) and 183 (Gold Coast) Squadrons forming No. 136 Wing. The ALG fairly pounded to the sound of Napier engines! They spent five days under canvas at Funtington before moving to Hurn and thence to France as a French Wing of 83 Group arrived from Merston on 22nd June to continue the tough offensive against the enemy. Nos. 329 (GC 1/2 'Cigognes'), 340 (GC IV/2 'Ile de France') and 341 (GC III/2 'Alsace') Squadrons with Spitfire IXs had a brief but successful stay at the ALG and moved on to Selsey on 1st July 1944.

Funtington was used by two other wings before its final closure. No. 135 Wing comprising Nos. 222 (Natal), 349 (Belgian) and 485 (RNZAF) Squadrons, all with Spitfire IXs carried out escort duties whilst at the ALG and they in turn were followed by No. 132 Wing with Nos. 66, 127, 331 (Norwegian) and 332 (Norwegian) Squadrons. Both wings stayed for two or three days before going on to Ford to prepare for the continent. The pace of the war was quickening all the time with the count-down to victory.

Funtington's career came to an end on 11th December 1944 when it was derequisitioned and clearance of the site began. The buildings and Blister hangars remained for some time after but today no sign is apparent that the site was ever used for anything but agriculture. It had served its purpose admirably and was soon lost to all but the historian.

Selsey

Not all of the ALGs in Sussex were the result of the 1942 surveys, for the occasional one had seen aviation long before the planned invasion of Europe. One such site was Selsey, five miles south of Chichester. The flat area of grassland running alongside the village of Church Norton had been used as a private airfield during the 1930s. On several occasions, Avro 504s had been seen sitting on the grass and it was assumed that these had flown over from Shoreham. The site had a hangar in the corner of the field and several little buildings, indicating that a club house or similar may have been built. The airfield ceased to exist at the outbreak of war and it was not until 1942 that someone, somewhere, remembered the little airfield at Selsey.

The plans for the ALG encompassed far more land than the original site and this immediately brought a lot of opposition from the Ministry of Agriculture who were overruled. The land was requisitioned in July 1942 and plans were made to lay Sommerfeld Track runways, the main one running NE/SW of 4,200 ft length and a secondary running SE/NW of 3,900 ft length. Work by an RAF construction unit began in February 1943 and was finished in time for No. 65 (East India) Squadron to fly their Spitfire VBs in from Fairlop on 31st May. 245 (Northern Rhodesian) Squadron also flew in from Fairlop two days later bringing their Typhoons to join the Spitfires. Together they formed No. 121 Airfield with the Spitfires undertaking mainly escort work whilst the Typhoons concentrated on further training interspersed with rocket attacks on enemy lines of communication. The month spent at Selsey ensured both 65 and 245 Squadrons were acclimatised to canvas living and operating from a basic airfield. They moved over to Kingsnorth and Lydd in Kent respectively whilst Selsey was upgraded in preparation for the coming 'Operation Overlord'.

Ready by 1st April 1944, No. 135 Airfield arrived with Nos. 485 (RNZAF), 222 (Natal) and 349 (Belgian) Squadrons. The motto of 349 was 'Strike hard – Strike Home' and this was never more appropriate than when they and the rest of 135 Airfield were operating from Selsey. Their Spitfire IXs were soon hard dive-bombing any available target in France together with many bomber escort sorties. On D Day proper, the squadrons were providing beach-head cover from dawn. No. 349 had a particularly satisfying day with two enemy aircraft shot down and a further three damaged. During an evening patrol on 8th July by all three squadrons, a large force of enemy aircraft were sighted and in the ensuing battle, seven of the enemy were claimed to have been shot down. Again on the 10th, No. 222 Squadron shot down two FW 190s for no loss to themselves whilst the New Zealanders became the first unit to refuel and rearm at a Normandy ALG.

It was back to dive-bombing operations for the wing from 19th June and a transfer to Coolham ALG on the 30th ensured that similar operations continued. Back to Selsey came Spitfire IXs, this time part of No. 145 (French) Wing consisting of Nos. 329, 340 and 341 Squadrons. Commanded by Wing Commander Crawford-Compton, they carried out escort missions and occasionally were briefed to attack Noball sites, achieving some success on 9th July when three ME 109s fell to the wing. The three French squadrons were briefly joined by No. 74 (Trinidad) Squadron on the 17th of the month but by 6th August, 145 Wing had left for the comfort of Tangmere and it was replaced by No. 135 Wing making a return visit to the ALG. Bomber escort duties were the main task of the wing this time but with the Allied progress in Europe, No. 33 Squadron went to B.10 ALG on 19th August whilst the rest of the wing headed for Tangmere.

For Selsey it was all over although permission to release the site was not given until March 1945. As usual, the runways were removed together with the hangars and the majority of the buildings, allowing nature to take over the rest. Today Selsey is a memory with nothing to remind us of a hectic few months.

The ALGs in Sussex played a very important part in the Allied push to victory. The experiencing of living in primitive conditions on primitive airfields was put to good use once the squadrons had moved to the continent. It was also good experience for the RE and RAF construction gangs who built the ALGs both here and on the continent. Their concentrated short term use ensured them a place in the history books.

There were a number of minor landing grounds in Sussex, of which only one saw service in any significant degree in World War Two.

Hammerwood

In 1940 the Army took over eight Plus D (90 hp Cirrus Minor) light planes for experiments in a new type of artillery spotting. As the experiments were successful, the type of work became known as Air Observation Post duties and for this purpose, British Taylorcraft produced the Auster I. The aircraft was a single engine, high wing three seat fabric covered aircraft with a cruising speed of 110 mph, ideal for the intended purpose. It first entered service in July 1942 with No. 651 Squadron at Old Sarum and as the need for AOP squadrons arose, several bases were set up in SE England to accommodate them.

One of the longer serving AOP bases was at Hammerwood near East Grinstead and indeed was often called by the latter. It consisted of a basic layout of two grass landing strips naturally camouflaged by the surrounding woodland. All the AOP bases were built to house units being prepared for the Second Front and included in these units

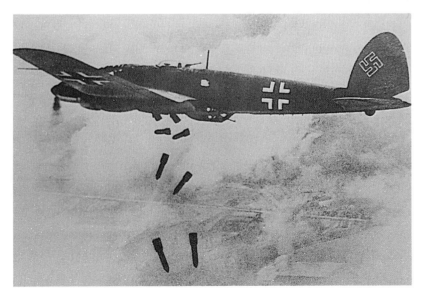

A HE 111 unloads its bombs over the UK. This twin-engined bomber was one of the workhorses of the Luftwaffe and was used extensively throughout the war (MAP).

165

was No. 660 Squadron who brought their Auster IIIs over from Andover on 20th November 1943. The squadron set up its headquarters in Hammerwood House and with detached flights of Austers operating from Holyte and Ashington, the rest of the aircraft began exercising with troops within the county.

The squadron experienced a very busy time whilst at Hammerwood, and in February 1944 their Mk. IIIs were exchanged for the Mk. IV. This aircraft introduced a third seat to the cockpit thus providing another person to navigate and carry out reconnaissance, for the aircraft, being very basic, was bereft of all navigational aids. As the Army pilots used to put it 'you fly this aircraft by the seat of your pants and good eyesight'. As the aircraft were flown by Army pilots and the groundcrews were all RAF, one can imagine the type of rivalry that sprang up between the 'brown jobs and the blue jobs'!

After continuing the artillery work through into the New Year, 660 Squadron left for Westernhangar on 23rd April 1944 and were replaced by No. 659 AOP Squadron the same day. The stayed at Hammerwood over the D Day period and moved with the Army to a landing strip at Cully in France on 14th June. No further use was found for the AOP squadrons in Sussex at this time and Hammerwood was returned to its owners. Though the AOP squadrons were operational after the war, Hammerwood was never again used.

10

CIVILIANS
AT WAR

The air war over Sussex had a profound effect on the civilian population. Since the first rumblings of war had been heard, the county had been gearing itself up for what everyone knew would ultimately happen. Air raid precautions had been discussed by local councils, some shelters had already appeared and the local talk was of what to do if and when the Germans invaded. The local weekly newspapers from 1938 onwards had been giving hints and advice but by the time war broke out in September 1939 many of the population did not know or did not care how to react in the event of an attack. It was thought that gas would be used as in the first conflict so everyone had been issued with a gas mask and told to make sure that they carried it everywhere. Very few heeded the advice and not until the Battle of Britain had begun did people take the threat of gas attacks and invasion seriously despite 38 million masks being issued.

Then came the blackout. For some months the local Sussex newspapers had been warning the people that should war come, one of the most effective ways of hindering enemy air attacks at night was to deny the pilots any lights on the ground. The first full test of a blackout took place in the county over the weekend of Saturday and Sunday 8th and 9th July 1939. It was planned that the RAF would fly over seven counties that weekend to observe just how effective the blackout was. On the ground, householders hung black material over every window, cars had hooded headlights and traffic lights were

London evacuees board a train to safety. As the 'phoney war' gave the country a false sense of security, many children returned to London, only to be faced with the horrors of the Blitz (South Eastern Newspapers).

With so many men on active service, volunteers were needed to help with farm work. For some, like these boy scouts, it was a healthy and enjoyable occupation — in good weather (Kent Messenger).

deflected downwards. Thirty minutes into the exercise the RAF had to return to base because of bad weather but there had been sufficient time to ascertain that the precautions were a success.

From January 1939 the air-raid siren system was regularly tested by the Civil Defence and Air Raid Precautions wardens. The recruiting of civilians not in the services for the forementioned organisations was going on at a fast pace, and regular meetings took place at drill halls all over the county. The best remembered voluntary body was the Home Guard, affectionately known as 'Dad's Army', which was first formed in May 1940 as the Local Defence Volunteers. Other civilians were employed on the airfields for such tasks as manning the boiler rooms, training military personnel in various jobs such as driving, or maintaining large vehicles. Most of the airfields were built by civilian labour and all of them retained a few tradesmen on a permanent basis for maintenance when they were completed. They became rather well known by the name of the 'works and bricks' department and did sterling work on airfields throughout the war. Another of the necessary civilian organisations to help and encourage the war effort was the NAAFI, beloved by all in the armed forces. Besides many of the Sussex airfields having a permanent brick built NAAFI, there was also the mobile 'tea wagon' to bring refreshment to many of the groundcrews working on the more lonely dispersal sites. Throughout the war it was that 'cup of tea' that kept up the morale of civilians and service personnel alike and the feeling was that everything would be all right after that 'cuppa'.

The mixture of civilians and military on the airfields, whilst generally good, did sometimes have its bad moments. One particular bone of contention was the British workman's habit of taking regular tea breaks and stopping work at precisely 5 pm. To the poor airmen working all hours often out in the wet and cold this was more than human suffering could bear and sometimes resulted in a very ungentlemanly exchange of words! The question of pay was another matter which caused problems. During one particular air-raid on Tangmere the civilian workers, fearing for their lives, downed tools at the first sound of the siren and rushed to the comparative safety of the nearest shelter. When the all-clear sounded they refused to leave the shelter and demanded an immediate wage increase to cover the risk to their lives. To the airmen who remained at their posts until the last possible moment, this was far too much and they attempted

A much loved, though sometimes maligned, institution was the NAAFI. Here a mobile van cheers RAF personnel with tea and a wad – service slang for a bun or roll (South Eastern Newspapers).

to smoke the civilian workers out of the shelter by lighting oily rags and stuffing them down the entrance. Only the threat of 'jankers' (detention) persuaded them to let the coughing civvies out!

Many of the airmen and WAAFS stationed in Sussex were billeted out at boarding houses in the area. There was a general feeling amongst them that some of the landlords and ladies were making as much money as they could in accommodating service personnel. Certainly conditions were far from comfortable with as many as three or four people living in one room with just a handbasin for washing purposes. Personal hygiene was at a premium, and entailed a weekly visit to the local municipal baths for either a shower or a bath. Food was generally another area of complaint and in fact many said that the conditions on the airfields themselves were superior to lodging out.

It was the bombing however that had the most devastating effect upon the entire civilian population. Generally people who had experienced a raid in which a bomb had either hit their house or

170

The constant air battles over Britain littered the country with the wreckage of both British and German planes. This grim scene shows the widely scattered remains of a British bomber which crashed in open countryside (South Eastern Newspapers).

landed next door would suffer a belated shock. Subsequent air raids would bring a feeling of nausea and the occasional uncontrollable shaking of the body. A parched feeling in the throat at the sound of whistling bombs as they fell and the urge to get outside into the open despite the obvious dangers were also signs of delayed shock. These feelings were to remain with many people until the end of the war, for long after the blitz had become a nightmarish memory, the hit and run raiders that attacked the Sussex towns were to bring out the same feelings of fear in the civilian population.

171

The Towns of Sussex at War

When it came to the number of air raids endured, Sussex was certainly a front line county. No town was spared the devastation and grief that each raid brought but it was obvious that some towns were to suffer more than others. During the Battle of Britain in 1940 and the blitz that came towards the end of 1940 and the beginning of 1941, it was the saturation bombing by the Germans that wrought such havoc. 1942 and 1943 saw the appearance of the hit and run raids by the fighter/bomber ME 109s and FW 190s known as Jabos. These were quick attacks carried out by fast aircraft carrying a single bomb. They usually flew low over the Channel to avoid detection by radar, then once over the coastline they attacked the towns by first dropping their bombs and then using cannon and machine gun fire as a follow up.

The worst single raid on Brighton was on a Saturday afternoon towards the end of the Battle of Britain. It was a bright sunny day and the lure of a good film at the local cinema at Kemp Town had attracted a full house. Suddenly out of a clear blue sky appeared the Luftwaffe who commenced to drop their bombs as they crossed the coastline. The cinema received a direct hit killing 55 people outright with many hundreds badly injured. The second worst incident was on 25th May 1943 at midday when 25 FW 190s dropped bombs and gunned the town indiscriminately leaving 24 people dead and 51 seriously injured. From July 1940 to March 1944, 56 air raids occurred within the Brighton borough leaving 198 civilians dead, 350 seriously injured and 433 slightly injured. A total of 381 high explosive bombs were dropped and the siren sounded 1,058 times. Such are the cold statistics of war!

Another town to suffer just as badly was Bexhill which received the first of its attacks on Wednesday 21st August 1940. Although the bomb fell on open farmland in the Lower Barnhorn Farm area causing no deaths or injuries, raids became almost a daily occurrence from this time during the Battle and the blitz. The morning of 19th September 1940 saw a particularly bad raid in the borough when bombs were dropped on the corner of Buckhurst Road and Sea Road. The explosion trapped two workmen and a gardener who were eventually dug out unharmed but the raid claimed one death. That

172

same day, two bombs were dropped and landed on some bungalows and houses in Barncroft Road. Two houses were demolished and many others made uninhabitable and two elderly ladies lost their lives. By 1944 the borough had received 51 air raids with 328 high explosive and 1,000 incendiary bombs being dropped. Twenty one civilians and one soldier were killed in these raids.

Very much smaller in size, East Grinstead probably suffered the county's worst tragedy. Although the town had been attacked during the Battle of Britain, there was no loss of life until Saturday 26th October 1940, the period in which the enemy was changing his tactics

A Gruppe of FW 190s ready for take-off. These are typical of the aircraft used for the hit and run raids on Sussex towns (MAP).

173

from the bombing of airfields to attacks on London and the bigger cities. At 9 pm on the Saturday evening, a lone raider appeared over the town and dropped a string of bombs along Holtye Road. They struck a large house trapping several people inside. They were eventually rescued and taken to the Queen Victoria Hospital nearby. This is the hospital made famous by the Guinea Pigs operations carried out by Archibald McIndoe, so named because the patients were really guinea pigs in this field. Many badly burnt aircrew owe their lives to this man who painstakingly put their burnt faces and limbs back together. Today it is still a very exclusive club known as the Guinea Pig Club though its roll of members is dwindling due the passage of time. One resident of the house, a nurse from the hospital, was killed in her bath as the bombs fell. It was however the incident which occurred at 5 pm on Friday 9th July 1943 that shook this town and the rest of the county so much.

In the late afternoon of that Friday, some ten aircraft crossed the

The bombing of Whitehall Cinema in East Grinstead was one of the most horrific attacks on civilians of the war. After the bombing the streets were strafed with machine gun fire (After the Battle).

Sussex coast at Hastings and headed for London. One raider detached himself from the main force and homed in on East Grinstead. It is thought that the pilot noticed a convoy of Army trucks stationary in the main car park just off the High Street, and circling the town twice, he released a stick of bombs within this area before once again circling the town. The Whitehall cinema just along the road from the car park received a direct hit and in the words of one of the survivors, 'the whole building seemed to collapse like a pack of cards, trapping most of the audience'. One hundred and eightyfour people were watching the film that evening when the air raid warning was flashed on the screen. Very few of them got up to leave, they had all previously experienced false alarms and thought this was another. The roof of the cinema split in two when the bomb came down and the entire structure caved in. Many people, adults and children, died instantly sitting in their seats. As the cinema continued to collapse the bomber came back and machine gunned the High Street. Bullets hit the walls of the burning buildings, the sound of the ricochet effect audible above the screaming and crying of the injured. Outside, the main road resembled a battlefield with bodies

Mourners at the mass grave in Mount Noddy Cemetery for 22 of the victims of the East Grinstead cinema bombing (After the Battle).

lying everywhere. By the time the emergency services arrived many of the buildings including the cinema were burning furiously. Whilst the AFS fought the flames, the Civil Defence together with servicemen and civilians began to dig away at the rubble with their bare hands in the hope of finding survivors. Later that night it was known that in all 108 people had died with a further 235 injured. It was the darkest hour East Grinstead had ever known. A mass funeral for 22 of the victims killed that day in the cinema was held on the following Wednesday at the Mount Noddy Cemetery in East Grinstead. It was a very melancholy affair and thousands of local people filed past the long grave placing flowers on the side. Even today each anniversary is marked by the laying of flowers along the entire length of the graves.

The town of Lewes was another Sussex town to be badly hit although one of the worst incidents came not during the Battle period but in 1943. At 12.30 pm on Wednesday 20th January, a force of six FW 190s from the 10th (Jabo) Staffel of JG 26 approached the town. They were detached from a larger force of about 34 aircraft that had taken advantage of the fact that the London balloon barrage had not been raised to carry out a horrific attack on the Capital. Coming in under the radar cover, the six left the main force as they crossed the coast and flying low over the town, dropped their 500 lb bombs at random. They caused widespread damage with one bomb landing at the top of North Street and killing a nine year old boy out on a shopping errand whilst another caused the death of an RAF man home on leave when it landed near West Street. It seemed as though the raid lasted only seconds; as the echoes of the explosions died away there were the sounds of falling masonry and the shouting of terrified people. Within minutes the services were on the scene aided by Canadian soldiers who were billeted at Lewes House on School Hill. Always eager to join in they gave sterling assistance in rescuing the buried and helping to retrieve personal belongings. As evening fell it was found that almost every building from St Michael's Clock to Cliffe Bridge had received some damage but luckily with very little personal injury. Every building, that is, with the exception of the Bull Inn, which remained open throughout to give succour and refreshment to the rescue services.

Lewes was not alone in its grief that day however. The rest of the Jabos that carried out the attack on the Capital were instrumental in

The grim aftermath of the hit and run raid on North Street, Lewes on 26 January 1943. The shock of the raid is evident from the demeanour of the people seen among the ruins (Bob Elliston, Eastbourne).

hitting a school in Catford, South East London. Sandhurst school was full of children whose ages ranged from 5 to 15 and at 12.30 pm that day they were all either sitting in their classrooms or eating lunch in the dining hall. With no air raid warning or alert being sounded they had no chance of taking cover before one of the aircraft dropped its bomb directly on the school killing 38 children and six teachers, with a further 60 children and several teachers badly wounded. The sheer randomness of the bombing by the Germans caused a public outcry and for days after, the national and local papers carried accounts of the outrage together with letters of sympathy from many countries. For Lewes and the Capital it was one of the blackest days of the war.

The most bombed town in Sussex was undoubtedly Eastbourne, which had found its popularity as the suntrap of the south coast in the 19th century. Its coastline looked across the Channel to enemy-held France, and upon its cliffs at Beachy Head was situated one of the early warning radars. It was possibly the siting of this that made Eastbourne such an attractive target to the Luftwaffe, yet despite

Eastbourne suffered the worst of the Sussex hit and run raids. The photograph shows the damage caused in Whitley Road. The part-wrecked house in the middle belonged to Miss Eileen Steel (Eileen Steel).

several raids elsewhere in the county the town was not subjected to a bad raid until Sunday 7th July 1940. Though a few days ahead of the now official beginning of the Battle of Britain on 10th July, it gave Eastbourne an indication of what was to come.

Whitley Road in Eastbourne was a largely residential area with general stores on several corners. Though the residents had heard the activity over the Channel convoys, only a few enemy aircraft as yet had strayed over the coastline. It was therefore something of a shock when a little after 10.30 am on that Sunday morning that an enemy aircraft, possibly a Dornier 17, was seen approaching Langney Point from the sea. The aircraft was observed through a pair of binoculars by Miss Eileen Steel, a resident of the road. Hearing the unfamiliar drone of the engines, she had rushed to an upstairs room to observe the intruder. Immediately the aircraft crossed the coast the ground batteries opened up and although their aim was not very accurate, the gunners did manage to persuade the pilot to change course from his intended target of the railway station to fly across Whitley Road.

178

Realising he would not reach the station he dropped his bombs at random, all of them landing in Whitley Road. Hearing the first crash further up the road, Eileen rushed to the top of her stairs intending to run down to the relative safety of her dining room table. Before she could get that far a bomb fell and hit the house next door. As the dust and rubble from her own ceiling fell around her she smelt the acrid stench of the explosive and the full impact of what was happening struck her. She tried to scream to release her emotions but no sound came. As the dust from the rubble cleared she went to the ground floor and gingerly opened her front door. It all seemed very quiet with the exception of people shouting and calling to each other. Coming out into the street she saw that the house next door had received a direct hit and was a pile of rubble. Everywhere was full of dust and the remnants of the house were still blazing as the timbers from the roof and the floorboards continued to burn. Miraculously the inhabitants, two women, had managed to crawl under their stairs when the raid began and this had protected them from the worst of the falling masonry. They escaped with broken limbs and lived to tell the tale. Not so fortunate were the occupants in other houses in Whitley Road who perished in the devastation.

When emergency services arrived the fire brigade immediately began to dowse the smouldering house and the air-raid wardens searched the rubble for further dead and injured. Fortunately at this early period of the war the bombs were not filled with extremely high explosive, but for this fact Eileen Steel would not have survived. By nightfall every inch of rubble had been searched and though no more bodies were found, the brigade and wardens remained in Whitley Road throughout the night. Together with many other residents of the road, Eileen helped to comfort the injured and bereaved and after 48 hours without sleep, returned to her own house counting her blessings.

During this early period of the war, many of the Eastbourne hotels were requisitioned by the military and were used to house soldiers and airmen of many nationalities including Polish, Czech and airmen of the Free French Squadrons. The Winter Gardens were used as a classroom to teach them basic English before they were sent for further training prior to joining a squadron. The evenings were free and the local dance halls and cinemas benefited greatly from their presence. Once again, Eileen Steel remembered the good times that were had by all and commented that even though the town was full of soldiers and airmen, one was never afraid to walk home alone in the blackout with just a glimmer of light from a dimmed torch.

The next few nights saw sporadic raids on coastal towns including Eastbourne and as the Battle of Britain increased in intensity, so did the raids on Sussex towns. Close proximity to an airfield or radar station ensured a raid and Eastbourne, situated between the radar stations at Pevensey and Beachy Head was a target that the Luftwaffe could not resist.

Contrary to popular belief, Beachy Head station was not one of the original Chain Home radar stations. When the first 20 were planned and completed by 1938, it was discovered that a gap in the radar cover existed at low level due to the curvature of the earth. A low flying aircraft could sometimes fly under the screen provided by the 20 stations and it was therefore imperative that a low radar screen was put into use as soon as possible. The first Chain Home Low, as they came to be called, was built at Foreness near Margate and was operational by 1939. By July 1940, the beginning of the Battle, Beachy Head and Fairlight near Hastings were on the air – the radar stations were operational – and the large aerials erected on the cliffs were almost beckoning the Luftwaffe 21 miles away across the Channel. It was therefore evident that a large town like Eastbourne would be an obvious target for heavy attacks.

Sunday 21st July 1940 saw a large collection of ships in the Channel travelling west. Codenamed 'Peewit', the convoy was sailing between Eastbourne and Bexhill when it became the subject of a large attack. It had been noted earlier in the afternoon that a lone Do 17 was carrying out a reconnaissance flight over the ships and was relaying messages back to its base in France. This induced the sector controller to scramble the Hurricanes of No. 238 Squadron from Middle Wallop in Hampshire. As a result F/O C Davis shot down the intruder although he himself later had to crash-land his aircraft due to enemy action. Thirty minutes later the main bomber force arrived over 'Peewit' and commenced their attack. In the ensuing battle, seven of the enemy were destroyed by the RAF with several damaged and the convoy survived. For the people of Eastbourne the battle provided an unusual Sunday afternoon's entertainment.

Another aspect of war in Eastbourne during 1940 was the nightly sound of the Luftwaffe laying mines in the Channel. Though of little

The job of clearing the wreckage of crashed planes fell to the military, with civilian help. The Sussex No. 1 Salvage Centre was at Faygate railway station, on the Chichester line (Imperial War Museum).

danger to the town, the sound alone made many residents nervous, automatically encouraging them to take to the shelters and cupboards under the stairs. Occasionally the noise of a ship striking a mine just offshore and the resulting explosion would light the coastline, again rekindling thoughts of an imminent invasion from across the Channel.

The second bad raid for Eastbourne came on Sunday 18th August, nowadays referred to as the 'hardest day' of the Battle of Britain. From early morning massed formations of German aircraft appeared overhead with every southern county seeing raids at one time or another. This final flourish was the end to the week-long effort of the Luftwaffe to destroy Fighter Command and once again it was the fighter airfields that were the main targets, with the towns taking the overspill. The might of Luftflotte 3 was massed against Sussex and

Hampshire in the afternoon, but from late morning, vast formations of enemy aircraft had been flying over Eastbourne heading for the Kent airfields. Later on it was the turn of the Stukas to attack Thorney Island and Ford with devastating results but several of the force preferred to drop their bombs on the towns with Eastbourne suffering most.

This then was the beginning of the raids that were to enable Eastbourne to acquire the distinctly unenviable title of the most raided town in the south east. The next three years were to see far more raids with fighter/bomber and high altitude attacks causing much greater damage than was caused during the Battle of Britain. With the main onslaught of the German offensive directly aimed at the towns and the civilian population, many people were killed or injured as a result. The FW 190 was to become a familiar sight during the years after the Battle, and later, during 1944, it was to be the V1 and V2 rockets that brought a reign of terror to Eastbourne and all of Sussex and Kent. Earlier in the war Mr Churchill had made one of his famous speeches in which he said, 'War is full of surprises, mostly unpleasant'. By the time the war was over, Eastbourne was bound to agree.

This chapter has described but a few of the tragedies that hit the county throughout the period of the war. The most visible reminders of the war on the towns are to be found in the many graveyards and cemeteries in the county, for as well as being a military war, it was also a people's war.

Appendix A

THE SQUADRONS OF THE ROYAL AIR FORCE THAT WERE BASED AT THE SUSSEX AIRFIELDS DURING AND AFTER WORLD WAR TWO

TANGMERE (3 miles ENE of Chichester) – 1, 14, 17, 25, 26, 29, 32, 34, 40, 41, 43, 65, 66, 69, 72, 74, 82, 85, 87, 91, 92, 96, 98, 115, 118, 124, 127, 129, 130, 131, 141, 145, 148, 164, 165, 183, 197, 198, 207, 208, 213, 217, 219, 222, 229, 233, 238, 245, 257, 266, 268, 302, 310, 312, 313, 329, 331, 332, 340, 341, 349, 501, 534, 587, 601, 605, 607, 609, 616.
WESTHAMPNETT (2 miles NE of Chichester) – 41, 65, 91, 118, 124, 129, 130, 31, 145, 174, 184, 245, 302, 303, 340, 350, 501, 602, 610, 616.
THORNEY ISLAND (8 miles ENE of Portsmouth) – 12, 22, 36, 42, 46, 48, 53, 56, 59, 63, 80, 86, 129, 130, 131, 143, 164, 193, 198, 217, 222, 233, 236, 248, 254, 278, 280, 547, 609, 612.
FORD (8 miles W of Chichester) – 10, 19, 22, 23, 29, 65, 66, 96, 97, 115, 122, 127, 132, 141, 144, 148, 149, 170, 215, 256, 302, 308, 315, 317, 331, 332, 602, 604, 605.
SHOREHAM (6 miles W of Brighton) – 14, 81, 82, 277, 345.
FRISTON (4 miles W of Eastbourne) – 32, 41, 64, 131, 253, 306, 308, 316, 349, 350, 501, 610.
MERSTON (2 miles SE of Chichester) – 41, 80, 118, 130, 131, 145, 174, 181, 182, 184, 229, 232, 247, 274, 303, 329, 340, 341.

In addition, many Fleet Air Arm squadrons were based at Ford during and after the Battle of Britain. There were also squadrons of the RCAF and RNZAF based at the airfields after the Battle of Britain.

Appendix B

THE SQUADRONS OF THE ROYAL AIR FORCE THAT WERE
BASED AT THE ADVANCED LANDING GROUNDS IN SUSSEX

APULDRAM (2 miles SSW of Chichester) – 175, 181, 302, 308, 310, 312, 313, 317.
BOGNOR (6 miles ESE of Chichester) – 19, 66, 122, 331, 332, 602.
CHAILEY (10 miles NNE of Brighton) – 302, 308, 317.
COOLHAM (6 miles SSW of Horsham) – 129, 222, 306, 315, 349.
DEANLAND (6 miles E of Lewes) – 64, 91, 234, 302, 308, 317, 322, 345, 611.
FUNTINGTON (4 miles WNW of Chichester) – 4, 19, 33, 65, 66, 122, 127, 164, 183, 198, 222, 268, 329, 331, 332, 340, 341, 349.
SELSEY (5 miles S of Chichester) – 65, 74, 222, 245, 329, 340, 341, 349, 485 (RNZAF).

Appendix C

THE MAIN LUFTWAFFE UNITS USED IN THE ASSAULT
ON THE AIRFIELDS
ORDER OF BATTLE – 13th AUGUST 1940

LUFTFLOTTE 2 – BRUSSELS – Commanded by Generalfeld-
marschall Albert Kesselring.
KAMPFGESCHWADER 1–2–3–4–40–53–76.
Equipment: Heinkel HE111 – Dornier DO17 – Focke Wulfe
FW200.
STUKAGESCHWADER 1.
Equipment: Junkers JU87B 'Stuka'.
LEHRGESCHWADER 1–2.
Equipment: Junkers JU87B 'Stuka' – Messerschmitt BF109E.
JAGDGESCHWADER 3–26–51–52–54.
Equipment: Messerschmitt BF109E.
ZERSTORERGESCHWADER 26–76.
Equipment: Messerschmitt BF110.
ERPROBUNGS GRUPPE 210 Messerschmitt BF109E –
Messerschmitt BF110.
KAMPFGRUPPE 100 – 106.
Equipment: Heinkel HE111.
KUSTENFLIEGERGRUPPE 106.
Equipment: Heinkel HE115 – Dornier DO18 – Junkers JU88D
– Heinkel 111.
LUFTFLOTTE 3 PARIS – Commanded by Generalfeldmarschall
Hugo Sperrle.
KAMPFGESCHWADER 1–27–51–54–55.
Equipment: Heinkel HE111 – Junkers JU88A.
STUKAGESCHWADER 1–2–3–77.
Equipment: Junkers JU87B 'Stuka' – Dornier DO17 – Heinkel
HE111.

LEHRGESCHWADER 1–2.
Equipment: Junkers JU88A – Messerschmitt BF110 – Dornier DO17F.
JAGDGESCHWADER 2–27–53.
Equipment: Messerschmitt BF109E.
ZERSTORERGESCHWADER 2.
Equipment: Messerschmitt BF110.
KAMPFGRUPPE 806.
Equipment: Junkers JU88 – Messerschmitt BF110 – Dornier DO17 – Henschell 126A.
In addition to the 2 main Luftflottes, Luftflotte 5 operated from Stavanger in Norway for attacks on east coast shipping and the east coast airfields.

Appendix D

GLOSSARY FOR LUFTWAFFE UNITS

Jagdgeschwader – Fighter Units
Kampfgeschwader – Bomber Units
Zerstorergeschwader – Long range fighter groups
Erprobungs Gruppe 210 – Experimental test wing 210
Lehrgeschwader – Instructional/operational development group
Stukageschwader – Dive bombing groups
Kustenfliegergruppe – Maritime Luftwaffe Units
Kampfgruppe – Coastal Units

GLOSSARY

ADGB	– Air Defence of Great Britain
AFS	– Auxiliary Fire Service
AI	– Airborne Interception
ASR	– Air Sea Rescue
ATC	– Air Traffic Control
BEF	– British Expeditionary Force
CIRCUS	– Fighter escorted bombing raid to attract the enemy
DIVER	– Operations against the V1 Rocket
ELG	– Emergency Landing Ground
FIU	– Fighter Interception Unit
GCI	– Ground Controlled Interception
E & RFTS	– Elementary and Reserve Flying Training School
MTB	– Motor Torpedo Boat
NAAFI	– Navy, Army and Air Force Institute
OCU	– Operational Conversion Unit
RAMROD	– Day bomber raid escorted by fighters
RANGER	– Deep penetration flights for targets of opportunity
RCAF	– Royal Canadian Air Force
RE	– Royal Engineers
RFC	– Royal Flying Corps
RHUBARB	– Low level strike operation carried out in occupied Europe
RNAS	– Royal Naval Air Service
RNVR	– Royal Naval Volunteer Reserve
RNZAF	– Royal New Zealand Air Force
ROADSTED	– Fighter operations against shipping
RODEO	– Fighter sweep
SOE	– Special Operations Executive
TAF	– Tactical Air Force
USAAF	– United States Army Air Force
Y SERVICE	– British secret listening service

BIBLIOGRAPHY

During my research I consulted various books. I list them below with grateful thanks to the authors.

RAF Squadrons – W/Cdr. C G Jefford (Airlife 1988)
Squadrons of the RAF – James J Halley (Air Britain 1980)
The Blitz – Then and Now, After the Battle – Winston G Ramsey (1987)
The Battle of Britain – Then and Now, After the Battle – Winston G Ramsey (1987)
Squadrons of the FAA – Ray Sturtivant (Air Britain 1984)
Action Stations – C Ashworth (Patrick Stephens 1985)
The Hardest Day – Alfred Price (Arms & Armour Press 1988)
Duel of Eagles – P Townsend (Weidenfeld & Nicolson 1990)
Eagle Day – Richard Collier (Hodder & Stoughton 1966)
Battle of Britain – Basil Collier (William Collins 1969)
Narrow Margin – D Wood and D Dempster (Hutchinson 1961)
Duel in the Sky – C Shores (Guild Publishing 1985)
Strike from the Sky – A McKee (Souvenir Press 1960)
Moon Squadron – Jerrard Tickell (Hodder & Stoughton 1960)
Fiasco – J Deane-Potter (William Heinemann 1970)
Fighter Command – C Bowyer (J M Dent & Sons 1980)
The First and the Last – Adolf Galland (Methuen & Co 1970)
Fleet Air Arm – (HMSO 1941)
Aircraft of The RAF – Owen Thetford (Putnam 1962)

ACKNOWLEDGEMENTS

I acknowledge with thanks all the organisations and individuals who gave me assistance in the writing of the book.

Andy Saunders of the Tangmere Military Aviation Museum Trust, Tony Moor of the Brenzett Aeronautical Museum, Phil Baldock of the Robertsbridge Aviation Society, Royal Air Force Museum – Hendon, Imperial War Museum, Fleet Air Arm Museum – Yeovilton, Alan Hibbett of Eastbourne Central Library, Brian Scott of Hastings Reference Library, Worthing Central Library, East Sussex Records Office – Lewes, Portsmouth Publishing and Printing Ltd, The West Sussex Gazette, Terry McCrae of the Truleigh Beautiful Aeroplane Company, Peter Campbell of Cirrus Associates, Mike Rice of Air Britain, Brighton Evening Argus, Miss Lindsey M. Hart of British Aerospace, No. 43 Squadron – RAF, 500 Squadron OCA, Public Record Office – Kew, Kent Messenger Newspaper, Len Pilkington, Ray Munday, Winston G. Ramsey, Miss Eileen Steel, KAHRS, Chris Samson and Bob Elliston.

The cover painting is copyright J. Salmon Ltd., Sevenoaks, Kent ©.

My special thanks go to Chris Samson for his excellent line drawings and to my wife Barbara for her work and patience.

If I have unknowingly omitted anyone or any organisation I offer my sincere apologies.

R.J.B.

INDEX

190

SQUADRONS

1 (RCAF) 16, 17, 35, 36, 38, 58, 59, 88
2 132
3 126
4 132, 160
13 122
17 51, 52
19 79, 153, 162
21 102, 103
22 85, 90, 91
23 56, 57, 59, 70, 71, 73
28 85
29 77, 78
30 146
32 43, 132, 133, 134
33 63, 164
41 59, 60, 61, 62, 117, 119, 122, 134, 135, 137, 142
42 84, 88, 91
43 17, 35, 36, 37, 38, 39, 40, 42, 43, 44, 45, 46, 47, 48, 50, 51, 52, 53, 54, 59, 69, 87, 88, 108, 126
48 56, 85
53 89, 91, 100
59 86, 88, 89, 90, 91, 98, 99, 100
61 17
64 43, 159
65 (East India) 55, 56, 79, 116, 117, 161, 163
66 60, 63, 82, 154, 162
73 40
74 (Trinidad) 43, 63, 164
80 145
83 60
84 (Typhoon Wing) 62
86 98
88 (Hong Kong) 72, 74
91 (Nigeria) 61, 62, 119, 159, 160
92 (East India) 17, 38
96 80, 82
107 73
118 60, 144
120 (Mysore) 116
122 (Bombay) 79, 153, 161
127 63, 82, 162
129 (Mysore) 81, 96, 97, 117, 156, 157
130 97
131 (County of Kent) 99, 119, 138, 141, 142, 155
141 74, 75
145 39, 40, 42, 43, 55, 69, 105, 107, 108, 109, 114, 141
148 18
152 88
161 62
164 (Argentine-British) 100, 101, 102, 162
167 (Gold Coast) 119
174 (Mauritius) 74, 77, 119, 143

175 119, 150, 151
181 & 182 144, 150, 151
183 (Gold Coast) 62, 63, 101, 102, 162
184 120, 122, 143
193 101
197 61, 62, 63
198 63, 102, 162
213 52, 55
217 36, 90, 91, 94, 96, 98
219 55, 56, 57, 59
222 (Natal) 64, 158, 162, 163, 164
225 132
229 145
234 (Madras Presidency) 159
235 86, 87, 88, 89, 90, 91
236 86
238 180
245 (Northern Rhodesian) 119, 126, 163
247 (China British) 144
253 (Hyderabad State) 126, 132, 133, 134
255 124
256 76, 77
266 (Rhodesia) 45, 63
268 160
274 145
277 58, 62, 126, 127, 128, 129, C Flight 125
278 103
280 91
302 (Poznan) 81, 113, 152, 155, 158
303 Kosciusko 81, 122, 146
306 (Torunski) 81, 135, 156, 157
308 Krakow 81, 152, 155, 158
310 63, 151
312 Wilenski 63, 150, 151, 152, 155
313 (Czech) 63
315 (Deblin) 81, 156, 157
316 (Warszawski) 137, 138
317 Wilno 81, 152, 158
322 (Dutch) 82, 159, 160
329 (GCI/2 Cignones) 145, 162, 164
331 63, 82
332 63, 154, 162
340 (Ile de France) 117, 145, 162, 164
341 (GCIII/2 Alsace) 145, 162, 164
345 (Free French) 128, 129, 159
349 (Belgian) 64, 135, 136, 158, 162, 163, 164
350 136
401 63
402 (Winnipeg Bear) 122, 143, 146
403 63
404 (Buffalo) 90
407 (Demon) 90

411 63
412 (Canadian) 60, 63, 134, 142
415 90, 91, 96, 99, 100
416 (City of Oshawa) 63, 143
418 (City of Edmonton) 74, 75
421 63
438 (Wild Cat) 161
439 (Westmount) 161
440 (City of Ottawa and Beaver) 161
441 (Silver Fox) 120, 161
442 (Caribou) 120, 161
443 (Hornet) 120, 161
456 78, 80, 81, 82
464 102
485 (RNZAF) 64, 119, 143, 158, 162, 163
486 (RNZAF) 60, 61, 62
487 102
489 (RNZAF) 96
501 (County of Gloucester) 38, 39, 60, 119, 136
502 98
547 100
601 39, 40, 41, 42, 44, 46, 48, 50, 51, 52, 88
602 (City of Glasgow) 109, 111, 112, 113, 153
604 (County of Middlesex) 75, 76
605 (County of Warwick) 36, 39, 73, 75
607 (County of Durham) 53, 54, 55
609 (West Riding) 63, 101, 102, 162
610 (County of Chester) 113, 114, 115, 116, 119, 122, 137
611 (West Lancs) 159
612 (County of Aberdeen) 98, 99
616 (South Yorkshire) 56, 113, 114, 115, 116, 118
651 165
659 AOP 166
660 166
666 (RCAF) 138
677 128
703 104
746 FAA 82
750, 751 & 752 66
810 103
812 88, 89
816 99
819 99
822 103
823 60
825 93
829 70
836 99, 100
838, 842, 848, 854, 855 103
1105 46
1622 Gosport 128